Letters from Iceland

W.H.AUDEN & LOUIS MacNEICE

Letters from Iceland

faber and faber

LONDON · BOSTON

First published in 1937
by Faber and Faber Limited
3 Queen Square London WC1N 3AU
First published in this edition in 1967
Reissued in 1985

Printed and bound by

Antony Rowe Ltd, Eastbourne

British Library Cataloguing in Publication Data

Auden, W.H.
Letters from Iceland.
1. Iceland – Description and travel
I. Title   II. MacNeice, Louis
914.91'2044   DL313
ISBN 0-571-13297-9

To
GEORGE AUGUSTUS AUDEN

Contents

Foreword

In April 1964, I revisited Iceland. Naturally, I expected
change, but the change was beyond all expectation.
During the last war, the island was occupied, first by the
British and then by the Americans. Military occupation,
no matter by whom, is never a pleasant business for the
occupied but, in the case of Iceland, it brought one
benefit. Meeting one of my old guides, now a school-
master, I asked him what life had been like during the
war. 'We made money,' he replied. And the prosperity
begun then has increased since Iceland became an
independent republic.

Reykjavik today is a very different place from the
rather down-at-heels town I remembered. In many cities,
modern architecture only makes one nostalgic for the old,
but in Reykjavik this is not so. Concrete, steel and glass
may not be one's favourite building materials, but they
are an improvement upon corrugated iron sheeting.

Those who wish to make strenuous treks through the
wilderness can still do so, but there are now more comfortable alternatives. There are roads everywhere, good but
not too good—no autobahns, thank God—and there is an
air-taxi service which will transport one quickly and
scenically to the most remote spots.

For the visitor, there is one loss. As I flew up to the
North-West to stay for three days at a farm where I had
stayed in 1936, I pictured to myself the pleasures of
riding in the afternoons. But the farmer had exchanged
his ponies for a Land-Rover. Sensible of him, but disap-

pointing for me. To-day, ponies are confined to tourist centres and riding, I should imagine, has become an expensive luxury.

For me personally, it was a joy to discover that, despite everything which had happened to Iceland and myself since my first visit, the feelings it aroused were the same. In my childhood dreams Iceland was holy ground; when, at the age of twenty-nine, I saw it for the first time, the reality verified my dream; at fifty-seven it was holy ground still, with the most magical light of anywhere on earth. Furthermore, modernity does not seem to have changed the character of the inhabitants. They are still the only really classless society I have ever encountered, and they have not—not yet—become vulgar.

Re-reading a book written half a lifetime ago has been an odd experience, and what readers under thirty will make of it I cannot imagine. Though writing in a 'holiday' spirit, its authors were all the time conscious of a threatening horizon to their picnic—world-wide unemployment, Hitler growing every day more powerful and a world-war more inevitable. Indeed, the prologue to that war, the Spanish Civil War, broke out while we were there.

Today, Louis MacNeice who wrote half the book and my father to whom it was dedicated are dead, the schoolboys with whom we went round the Langjökul husbands and fathers, and many of the "recipients" of our Letters public figures—A Cabinet Minister, a knight, a television star, etc.

In the parts which I wrote, I have made some cuts and revisions. One chapter jointly written, *Last Will and Testament*, seems to me excessively private in its jokes, and I wondered whether I oughtn't to cut it. But American friends to whom all the Proper Names are unknown have told me that they enjoyed it, so I have left it as it was.

As to the merits of the book, if any, I am in no position to judge. But the three months in Iceland upon which it is based stand out in my memory as among the happiest in a life which has, so far, been unusually happy, and, if something of this joy comes through the writing, I shall be content.

W. H. AUDEN, 1965

Preface

A travel book owes so little to the writers, and so much to the people they meet, that a full and fair acknowledgment on the part of the former is impossible.

We must beg those hundreds of anonymous Icelanders, farmers, fishermen, busmen, children, etc., who are the real authors of this book to accept collectively our gratitude. In particular we should like to thank The Icelandic Shipping Co., The Stat-Tourist Bureau, Mr. and Mrs. Eirikur Benedikz, Mr. Olafur Briem, Mr. Ragnar Jonasson, Professor Sigurdur Nordal and Professor Arni Pällsson of Reykjavik University, Dr. Jonas Lárusson and Dr. Gislisson of the Studentagardur, Mr. and Mrs. Kristjan Andresson, Mr. Stefan Stefansson, Mr. Snaebjorn Jonsson, Mr. and Mrs. Little, Mr. Atli Olafson, Mr. Halldor Laxness, Mr. Tomas Gudmundsson, Dr. Sorenson, Mr. Thorbjorn Thordarson, Dr. Kristiansson of Sandakrökur, Mr. Bjarkans of Akureyri, Mr. Gerry Pällsson, our two guides Stengrimur and Ari (we never found out their other name), Mr. Joachimsson of Isafjordur, Mr. Gudmundur Hagalin, and Dr. Sveinsson and family, to whom we must also apologise for entirely destroying a bed.

Lastly we must express our gratitude to Professor E. V. Gordon for invaluable introductions and advice, and to Mr. Michael Yates for his company and the use of his diary.

W.H.A.
L.M.

Chapter I

Letter to Lord Byron

———————

PART I

Excuse, my lord, the liberty I take
    In thus addressing you. I know that you
Will pay the price of authorship and make
    The allowances an author has to do.
    A poet's fan-mail will be nothing new.
And then a lord—Good Lord, you must be peppered,
Like Gary Cooper, Coughlin, or Dick Sheppard,

With notes from perfect strangers starting, 'Sir,
    I liked your lyrics, but *Childe Harold's* trash',
'My daughter writes, should I encourage her?'
    Sometimes containing frank demands for cash,
    Sometimes sly hints at a platonic pash,
And sometimes, though I think this rather crude,
The correspondent's photo in the rude.

And as for manuscripts—by every post . . .
    I can't improve on Pope's shrill indignation,
But hope that it will please his spiteful ghost
    To learn the use in culture's propagation
    Of modern methods of communication;
New roads, new rails, new contacts, as we know
From documentaries by the G.P.O.

15

For since the British Isles went Protestant
    A church confession is too high for most.
But still confession is a human want,
    So Englishmen must make theirs now by post
    And authors hear them over breakfast toast.
For, failing them, there's nothing but the wall
Of public lavatories on which to scrawl.

So if ostensibly I write to you
    To chat about your poetry or mine,
There're many other reasons; though it's true
    That I have, at the age of twenty-nine
    Just read *Don Juan* and I found it fine.
I read it on the boat to Reykjavik
Except when eating or asleep or sick.

Now home is miles away, and miles away
    No matter who, and I am quite alone
And cannot understand what people say,
    But like a dog must guess it by the tone;
    At any language other than my own
I'm no great shakes, and here I've found no tutor
Nor sleeping lexicon to make me cuter.

The thought of writing came to me to-day
    (I like to give these facts of time and space);
The bus was in the desert on its way
    From Mothrudalur to some other place:
    The tears were streaming down my burning face;
I'd caught a heavy cold in Akureyri,
And lunch was late and life looked very dreary.

Professor Housman was I think the first
    To say in print how very stimulating
The little ills by which mankind is cursed,
    The colds, the aches, the pains are to creating;

Indeed one hardly goes too far in stating
That many a flawless lyric may be due
Not to a lover's broken heart, but 'flu.

But still a proper explanation's lacking;
Why write to you? I see I must begin
Right at the start when I was at my packing.
The extra pair of socks, the airtight tin
Of China tea, the anti-fly were in;
I asked myself what sort of books I'd read
In Iceland, if I ever felt the need.

I can't read Jefferies on the Wiltshire Downs,
Nor browse on limericks in a smoking-room;
Who would try Trollope in cathedral towns,
Or Marie Stopes inside his mother's womb?
Perhaps you feel the same beyond the tomb.
Do the celestial highbrows only care
For works on Clydeside, Fascists, or Mayfair?

In certain quarters I had heard a rumour
(For all I know the rumour's only silly)
That Icelanders have little sense of humour.
I knew the country was extremely hilly,
The climate unreliable and chilly;
So looking round for something light and easy
I pounced on you as warm and civilisé.

There is one other author in my pack:
For some time I debated which to write to.
Which would least likely send my letter back?
But I decided that I'd give a fright to
Jane Austen if I wrote when I'd no right to,
And share in her contempt the dreadful fates
Of Crawford, Musgrave, and of Mr. Yates.

Then she's a novelist. I don't know whether
    You will agree, but novel writing is
A higher art than poetry altogether
    In my opinion, and success implies
    Both finer character and faculties.
Perhaps that's why real novels are as rare
As winter thunder or a polar bear.

The average poet by comparison
    Is unobservant, immature, and lazy.
You must admit, when all is said and done,
    His sense of other people's very hazy,
    His moral judgments are too often crazy,
A slick and easy generalisation
Appeals too well to his imagination.

I must remember, though, that you were dead
    Before the four great Russians lived, who brought
The art of novel writing to a head;
    The help of Boots had not been sought.
    But now the art for which Jane Austen fought,
Under the right persuasion bravely warms
And is the most prodigious of the forms.

She was not an unshockable blue-stocking;
    If shades remain the characters they were,
No doubt she still considers you as shocking.
    But tell Jane Austen, that is, if you dare,
    How much her novels are beloved down here.
She wrote them for posterity, she said;
'Twas rash, but by posterity she's read.

You could not shock her more than she shocks me;
    Beside her Joyce seems innocent as grass.
It makes me most uncomfortable to see

An English spinster of the middle-class
    Describe the amorous effects of 'brass',
Reveal so frankly and with such sobriety
The economic basis of society.

So it is you who is to get this letter.
    The experiment may not be a success.
There're many others who could do it better,
    But I shall not enjoy myself the less.
    Shaw of the Air Force said that happiness
Comes in absorption: he was right, I know it;
Even in scribbling to a long-dead poet.

Every exciting letter has enclosures,
    And so shall this—a bunch of photographs,
Some out of focus, some with wrong exposures,
    Press cuttings, gossip, maps, statistics, graphs;
    I don't intend to do the thing by halves.
I'm going to be very up to date indeed.
It is a collage that you're going to read.

I want a form that's large enough to swim in,
    And talk on any subject that I choose,
From natural scenery to men and women,
    Myself, the arts, the European news:
    And since she's on a holiday, my Muse
Is out to please, find everything delightful
And only now and then be mildly spiteful.

Ottava Rima would, I know, be proper,
    The proper instrument on which to pay
My compliments, but I should come a cropper;
    Rhyme-royal's difficult enough to play.
    But if no classics as in Chaucer's day,
At least my modern pieces shall be cheery
Like English bishops on the Quantum Theory.

Light verse, poor girl, is under a sad weather;
    Except by Milne and persons of that kind
She's treated as démodé altogether.
    It's strange and very unjust to my mind
    Her brief appearances should be confined,
Apart from Belloc's *Cautionary Tales*,
To the more bourgeois periodicals.

'The fascination of what's difficult,'
    The wish to do what one's not done before,
Is, I hope, proper to Quicunque Vult,
    The proper card to show at Heaven's door.
    'Gerettet' not 'Gerichtet' be the Law,
Et cetera, et cetera. O curse,
That is the flattest line in English verse.

Parnassus after all is not a mountain,
    Reserved for A.1. climbers such as you;
It's got a park, it's got a public fountain.
    The most I ask is leave to share a pew
    With Bradford or with Cottam, that will do:
To pasture my few silly sheep with Dyer
And picnic on the lower slopes with Prior.

A publisher's an author's greatest friend,
    A generous uncle, or he ought to be.
(I'm sure we hope it pays him in the end.)
    I love my publishers and they love me,
    At least they paid a very handsome fee
To send me here. I've never heard a grouse
Either from Russell Square or Random House.

But now I've got uncomfortable suspicions,
    I'm going to put their patience out of joint.
Though it's in keeping with the best traditions

For Travel Books to wander from the point
(There is no other rhyme except anoint),
They well may charge me with—I've no defences—
Obtaining money under false pretences.

I know I've not the least chance of survival
    Beside the major travellers of the day.
I am no Lawrence who, on his arrival,
    Sat down and typed out all he had to say;
    I am not even Ernest Hemingway.
I shall not run to a two-bob edition,
So just won't enter for the competition.

And even here the steps I flounder in
    Were worn by most distinguished boots of old.
Dasent and Morris and Lord Dufferin,
    Hooker and men of that heroic mould
    Welcome me icily into the fold;
I'm not like Peter Fleming an Etonian,
But, if I'm Judas, I'm an old Oxonian.

The Haig Thomases are at Myvatn now,
    At Hvitavatn and at Vatnajökull
Cambridge research goes on, I don't know how:
    The shades of Asquith and of Auden Skökull
    Turn in their coffins a three-quarter circle
To see their son, upon whose help they reckoned,
Being as frivolous as Charles the Second.

So this, my opening chapter, has to stop
    With humbly begging everybody's pardon.
From Faber first in case the book's a flop,
    Then from the critics lest they should be hard on
    The author when he leads them up the garden,
Last from the general public he must beg
Permission now and then to pull their leg.

END OF PART I

Chapter II

Journey to Iceland

A letter to Christopher Isherwood, Esq.

And each traveller hopes: 'Let me be far from any
Physician.' And each port has a name for the sea,
 The citiless, the corroding, the sorrow.
 And North means to all: 'Reject!'

The great plains are for ever where the cold fish are
 hunted
And everywhere. Light birds flicker and flaunt:
 Under a scolding flag the lover
 Of islands may see at last,

Faintly, his limited hope, as he nears the glitter
Of glaciers, the outlines of sterile mountains, intense
 In the abnormal day of this world, and a river's
 Fan-like polyp of sand.

Then let the good citizen find here natural marvels:
A horse-shoe ravine, the issue of steam from a cleft
 In the rock, and rocks, and waterfall brushing the
 Rocks, and, among the rocks, birds.

The student of prose and conduct find places to visit:
The site of a church where a bishop was put in a bag,
 The bath of a great historian, the rock where
 An outlaw dreaded the dark.

Remember the doomed man thrown by his horse and
 crying:
'Beautiful is the hillside, I will not go.';
 The old woman confessing: 'He that I loved the
 Best, to him I was worst.'

Islands are places apart where Europe is absent.
Are they? The world still is, the present, the lie,
 And the narrow bridge over a torrent
 Or the small farm under a crag

Are natural settings for the jealousies of a province:
A weak vow of fidelity is sworn by the cairn,
 And within the indigenous figure on horseback
 On the bridle-path down by the lake

The blood moves also by crooked and furtive inches,
Asks all our questions: 'Where is the homage? When
 Shall justice be done? O who is against me?
 Why am I always alone?'

For our time has no favourite suburb: no local features
Are those of the young for whom all wish to care:
 The promise is only a promise, the fabulous
 Country impartially far.

Tears fall in all the rivers. Again a driver
Pulls on his gloves and in a blinding snowstorm starts
 Upon his deadly journey: again some writer
 Runs howling to his art.

Dear Christopher,

Thank you for your letter. No, you were wrong. I did not write: 'the *ports* have names for the sea' but 'the *poets* have names for the sea'. However, as so often before, the mistake seems better than the original idea, so I'll leave it. Now, as to your questions:

1. 'I can't quite picture your arrival. What was your impression of Reykjavik harbour? Is there any attempt to make the visitor feel that he is arriving at a capital city?'

Not much. There is nothing by the pier but warehouses and piles of agricultural implements under tarpaulin. Most of the town is built of corrugated iron. When we arrived, it was only half-past seven and we had to wait outside the harbour, because the Icelandic dockhands won't get up early. The town was hidden in low-lying mist, with the tops of the mountains showing above it. My first impression of the town was Lutheran, drab and remote. The quay was crowded with loungers, passively interested, in caps. They seemed to have been there a long time. There were no screaming hawkers or touts. Even the children didn't speak.

2. 'What does R. look like?'

There is no good building stone. The new suburban houses are built of concrete in sombre colours. The three chief buildings are the Roman Catholic church, the (unfinished) theatre and the students' hostel, which looks like waiting-rooms of an airport. There is a sports ground, with a running-track and tennis courts, where the young men play most of the night. In the middle of the town there is a shallow artificial lake full of terns and wild duck. The town peters out into flat rusty-brown lava-fields, scattered shacks surrounded by wire-fencing, stockfish drying on washing-lines and a few white hens. Further down the coast, the lava is dotted with what look like huge laundry-baskets; these are really compact heaps of drying fish covered with tarpaulin. The weather changes with extraordinary rapidity: one moment the rain blots out everything, the next, the sun is shining behind clouds, filling the air with an intense luminous light in which you can see for miles, so that every detail of the cone-shaped mountains stands out needle-sharp against an orange sky. There is one peak which is always bright pink.

3. 'What do the Icelandic authors write about?'

Mainly about their own country, the emotional lives of the farmers and fishermen and their struggle with nature.

4. 'I suppose the originals of the fiction-characters are generally well-known?'

Yes, often. I sometimes heard complaints; for example, that Halldor Laxness makes the farmers more unpleasant than they really are. But, as far as I could gather, there are no laws of libel.

5. 'Isn't the audience of the Icelandic novelist very small?'

Relatively to the size of the population, it is larger than in most countries. Most of the novels of any standing are translated into German and the other Scandinavian languages.

6. 'Can he make a living?'

The best-known authors and painters receive support from the state, without any obligations as to output. People (in all cases, right wing) occasionally complained to me that politics influenced the awards; but I couldn't discover any authors of merit who had been neglected.

7. 'Tell me about the young Icelander. What does he think about? What are his ambitions?'

As a race, I don't think the Icelanders are very ambitious. A few of the professional classes would like to get to Europe; most would prefer to stay where they are and make a certain amount of money. Compared with most countries, there is little unemployment in Iceland. My general impression of the Icelander is that he is realistic, in a petit bourgeois sort of way, unromantic and unidealistic. Unlike the German, he shows no romantic longing for the south, and I can't picture him in a uniform. The attitude to the sagas is like that of the average Englishman to Shakespeare; but I only found one man, a painter, who dared to say he thought they were 'rather rough'. The difficulty of getting any job at all in many European countries tends to make the inhabitants irresponsible and therefore ready for fanatical patriotism; but the Icelander is seldom irresponsible, because irresponsibility in a farmer or fisherman would mean ruin.

8. 'What about the sex-life?'

Uninhibited. There is little stigma attached to illegitimacy. Bastards are brought up on an equal footing with legitimate children of the family. Before communications became better, there was a good deal of in-breeding. A farmer was pointed out to me who had married his niece, by special permission of the King of Denmark. Homosexuality is said to be rare. There is a good deal of venereal disease in the coastal towns, which has lately begun to spread inland. I know nothing about birth-control propaganda: there seems to be no particular drive to increase the population of the island. Emigration to America, which was common at the beginning of the century, has now stopped.

9. 'Is there a typical kind of Icelandic humour?'

They are very fond of satirical lampoons. As you would expect on a small island, most of the jokes are about prominent personalities and difficult to understand without inside knowledge. There is a weekly comic paper called the *Spegelin*, which is more like *Simplicissimus* than like *Punch*. I saw no evidence of the kind of brutal practical joke practised in the sagas.

10. 'What feelings did your visit give you about life on

small islands?'

If you have no particular intellectual interests or ambitions and are content with the company of your family and friends, then life on Iceland must be very pleasant, because the inhabitants are friendly, tolerant and sane. They are genuinely proud of their country and its history, but without the least trace of hysterical nationalism. I always found that they welcomed criticism. But I had the feeling, also, that for myself it was already too late. We are all too deeply involved with Europe to be able, or even to wish to escape. Though I am sure you would enjoy a visit as much as I did, I think that, in the long run, the Scandinavian sanity would be too much for you, as it is for me. The truth is, we are both only really happy living among lunatics.

W.

Chapter III

Letter to Graham and Anne Shepard

————————

Reykjavik.
August 16*th*, 1936.

To Graham and Anna: from the Arctic Gate
I send this letter to N.W. 8,
Hoping that Town is not the usual mess,
That Pauli is rid of worms, the new cook a success.
I have got here, you see, without being sick
On a boat of eight hundred tons to Reykjavik.
Came second-class—no air but many men;
Having seen the first-class crowd would do the same again.
Food was good, mutton and bits of fishes,
A smart line-up of Scandinavian dishes—
Beet, cheese, ham, jam, smoked salmon, gaffalbitar,
Sweet cucumber, German sausage, and Rye-Vita.
So I came here to the land the Romans missed,
Left for the Irish saint and the Viking colonist.
But what am I doing here? Qu'allais-je faire
Among these volcanic rocks and this grey air?
Why go north when Cyprus and Madeira
De jure if not de facto are much nearer?
The reason for hereness seems beyond conjecture,
There are no trees or trains or architecture,
Fruits and greens are insufficient for health
And culture is limited by lack of wealth,

Letter to Graham and Anne Shepard

The tourist sights have nothing like Stonehenge,
The literature is all about revenge.
And yet I like it if only because this nation
Enjoys a scarcity of population
And cannot rise to many bores or hacks
Or paupers or poor men paying Super-Tax.
Yet further, if you can stand it, I will set forth
The obscure but powerful ethics of Going North.
Morris did it before, dropping the frills and fuss,
Harps and arbours, Tristram and Theseus,
For a land of rocks and sagas. And certain unknown
Old Irish hermits, holy skin and bone,
Camped on these crags in order to forget
Their blue-black cows in the Kerry pastures wet.
Those Latin-chattering margin-illuminating monks
Fled here from home without kit-bags or trunks
To mortify their flesh—but we must mortify
Our blowsy intellects before we die,
Who feed our brains on backchat and self-pity
And always need a noise, the radio or the city,
Traffic and changing lights, crashing the amber,
Always on the move and so do not remember
The necessity of the silence of the islands,
The glacier floating in the distance out of existence,
The need to grip and grapple the adversary,
Knuckle on stony knuckle, to dot and carry
One and carry one and not give up the hunt
Till we have pinned the Boyg down to a point.
In England one forgets—in each performing troupe
Forgets what one has lost, there is no room to stoop
And look along the ground, one cannot see the ground
For the feet of the crowd, and the lost is never found.
I dropped something, I think, but I am not sure what
And cannot say if it mattered much or not,
So let us get on or we shall be late, for soon

Letter to Graham and Anne Shepard

The shops will close and the rush-hour be on.
This is the fret that makes us cat-like stretch
And then contract the fingers, gives the itch
To open the French window into the rain,
Walk out and never be seen at home again.
But where to go? No oracle for us,
Bible or Baedeker, can tell the terminus.
The songs of jazz have told us of a moon country
And we like to dream of a heat which is never sultry,
Melons to eat, champagne to drink, and a lazy
Music hour by hour depetalling the daisy.
Then Medici manuscripts have told of places
Where common sense was wedded to the graces,
Doric temples and olive-trees and such,
But broken marble no longer goes for much.
And there are some who scorn this poésie de départs
And say 'Escape by staying where you are;
A man is what he thinks he is and can
Find happiness within.' How nice to be born a man.
The tourist in space or time, emotion or sensation,
Meets many guides but none have the proper orientation.
We are not changing ground to escape from facts
But rather to find them. This complex world exacts
Hard work of simplifying; to get its focus
You have to stand outside the crowd and caucus.
This all sounds somewhat priggish. You and I
Know very well the immediate reason why
I am in Iceland. Three months ago or so
Wystan said that he was planning to go
To Iceland to write a book and would I come too;
And I said yes, having nothing better to do.
But all the same we never make any choice
On such a merely mechanical stimulus.
The match is not the cause of fire, so pause
And look for the formal as well as the efficient cause.

Letter to Graham and Anne Shepard

Aristotle's pedantic phraseology
Serves better than common sense or hand to mouth psycho-
    logy.
'ἔσχε τὴν φύσιν'—'found its nature'; the crude
Embryo rummages every latitude
Looking for itself, its nature, its final pattern,
Till the fairy godmother's wand touches the slattern
And turns her to a princess for a moment
Beyond definition or professorial comment.
We find our nature daily or try to find it,
The old flame gutters, leaves red flames behind it.
An interval of tuning and screwing and then
The symphony restarts, the creature lives again—
Blake's arabesques of fire; the subtle creature
Swings on Ezekiel's wheels, finding its nature.
In short we must keep moving to keep pace
Or else drop into Limbo, the dead place.
I have come north, gaily running away
From the grinding gears, the change from day to day,
The creaks of the familiar room, the smile
Of the cruel clock, the bills upon the file,
The excess of books and cushions, the high heels
That walk the street, the news, the newsboys' yells,
The flag-days and the cripple's flapping sleeve,
The ambushes of sex, the passion to retrieve
Significance from the river of passing people,
The attempt to climb the ever-climbing steeple
And no one knows what is at the top of it,
All is a raffle for caps which may not fit,
But all take tickets, keep moving; still we may
Move off from movement or change it for a day;
Here is a different rhythm, the juggled balls
Hang in the air—the pause before the soufflé falls.
Here we can take a breath, sit back, admire
Stills from the film of life, the frozen fire;

Letter to Graham and Anne Shepard

Among these rocks can roll upon the tongue
Morsels of thought, not jostled by the throng,
Or morsels of un-thought, which is still better,
(Thinking these days makes a suburban clatter).
Here we can practise forgetfulness without
A sense of guilt, fear of the tout and lout,
And here—but Wystan has butted in again
To say we must go out in the frightful rain
To see a man about a horse and so
I shall have to stop. For we soon intend to go
Around the Langjökull, a ten days' ride,
Gumboots and stockfish. Probably you'll deride
This sissy onslaught on the open spaces.
I can see the joke myself; however the case is
Not to be altered, but please remember us
So high up here in this vertiginous
Crow's-nest of the earth. Perhaps you'll let us know
If anything happens in the world below?

L. M.

Chapter IV
For Tourists

Passports, Customs, etc.

No passports are required for Iceland. There are duties on most of the customary articles but the customs examination on board is courteous and not vigorous.

Currency

Icelandic currency is reckoned in kronur and öre, 100 öre to the kronur. The official rate of exchange in Iceland in summer 1936 was 22.15 kr. to the pound. But in Hull you could get 24.50. It is better therefore not to change money officially. Owing to the adverse trade balance it is extremely difficult for individual Icelanders to get English currency, and English people who have friends or acquaintances in Iceland will be doing them a great service if they change their money with them.

Travellers' cheques can of course be used, but in my experience, it is wiser to take cash and change it as you want it, so that you are not landed at the end of your visit with a lot of Icelandic currency which is difficult to dispose of.

Clothes and Equipment

(1) The most essential article is a pair of stout gumboots, but with smooth soles or they get caught in the stirrups.

Riding-boots will be ruined and will not keep you dry. At least two pairs of socks should be worn inside the gumboots. A pair of walking shoes and a pair of slippers or gym-shoes will complete the foot-gear.

(2) For riding, either riding-breeches or plus-fours let down to the ankle.

(3) Oilskin trousers in one piece reaching to the waist.

(4) A long oilskin coat coming down well below the knees. A cape is useless.

(5) An oilskin sou'-wester as well as any other head-gear.

(6) A pair of warm but flexible gloves.

(7) As far as general clothing is concerned, the danger is of putting on too little rather than too much. On expeditions I always wore flannel trousers and pyjamas under my riding breeches, and two shirts and a golf-jacket and a coat under my oilskin. (So W.H.A. I did not wear nearly as much as this. L. M.)

(8) For expeditions into the interior, a tent, of course, is required. Make sure that your sleeping-bag is warm enough. It is wise perhaps to take a compass, but the mountains are sometimes magnetic and derange them. Air-tight tins for perishable food should be taken, and make sure that your stove is strong enough to stand up to the jolting it will get on a pack horse. Mine fell to pieces. In dry weather the lava dust can be very tiresome to the eyes, and it is a good thing to take a pair of tinted glasses. Finally, whether camping or not, a roll of toilet paper is invaluable.

(9) Everyone has their pet medicines, but from personal experience I would recommend chlorodyne as the best stuff to take in cases of internal disorder. Before I went, I heard a lot about mosquitoes, and went prepared. This is unnecessary. There are, I believe, mosquitoes at Myvatn, but elsewhere one need have no anxiety. In cases of emergency there are reliable doctors and dentists.

For Tourists

Maps, etc.

The best general map of the whole island is Daniel Bruun's, which gives all roads and footpaths and also camping sites. The whole island is being mapped in 8 sheets on a scale of a little over four miles to the inch. So far four sheets have appeared: South-West, Mid-West, North-West, and Mid-North. There are also special larger-scale sheets of special areas, like Thingvellir and Myvatn. All the inhabited part of the island is to be done on a scale of 1-100,000 but only some have appeared. All these maps can be bought in Reykjavik. The best guide book is *Iceland for Tourists* by Stefan Stefansson.

Boats to Iceland

The Icelandic Steam Shipping Company run two boats, the *Gullfoss* and the *Bruarfoss*, from Leith, and two, the *Godafoss* and the *Dettifoss*, from Hull. As far as the second-class accommodation goes, it is better on the Hull boats and best on the *Dettifoss*. Fare from Hull to anywhere in Iceland, £4 10s. plus 5 kr. a day for food. The latter is nothing to write home about but eatable. The voyage should last 4½ days, but delays in starting and on the way are quite probable. In addition, of course, there are cruise boats like the Danish *Primula*, with first-class accommodation only, which also call at the Faroes. *Primula* fare: £8, plus 8s. a day for food. An alternative route, for those who like the sea, is to go to Bergen and take a Norwegian boat from there, either the *Lyra* which goes to the Faroes and Reykjavik, or the *Nova* which goes direct to Eskifjördur and then slowly northward round the coast to Reykjavik. During the season it is wise to book both the outward and the return journey some time beforehand as accommodation is limited.

The Icelandic boats go on from Reykjavik west and north via Isafjördur to Akureyri and then back to Reykjavik.

For Tourists

Reykjavik

There is not much to be said for Reykjavik. The six hotels are The Borg, The Island, The Skjalbreid, the Vik, the Hekla, and the Studentagardur. The Borg is called a first-class hotel but is not the kind of thing you like if you like that kind of thing; still it is the only place where you can get a drink. As far as rooms, price, and general comfort go, unquestionably the best place to stay is the Studenta-gardur, though I think the food there could be better. Price 10 kr. a day inclusive (except for laundry) plus 10% for service. Single meals (lunch or dinner) cost from 2.50 kr. to 6 kr. There is a café in the Ausserstraeti where you can get decent cream cakes. The Borg has a jazz band and dancing every evening. There are two cinemas and two quite decent bookshops. Arrangements for expeditions, guides, horses, etc., are made through the Stat-Tourist bureau near the harbour. In the museum (open Wednesdays and Sundays) there is a remarkable painting on wood of the Last Supper which is worth seeing, and there is a collection of Icelandic paintings in the Parliament house. The Einar Jonsson museum is not for the fastidious. The only other sights are Olli Maggadon at the harbour, Oddur Sigurgeirsson anywhere, Kjarval the painter, and Arni Pállsson the professor of Icelandic history.

Board and Lodging

Nearly every farm will put you up, and though the standard of comfort of course varies, they will all do their best to make you comfortable. Prices from 4 to 6 kr. a day inclusive. In the N.W. it is a little cheaper. At a farm in the Isafjördardjup, for example, I paid 10 kr. for three days including riding. Single meals (lunch and dinner), 2 kr. In the summer many of the schools in the country are turned into hotels, *e.g.* Laugarvatn, Reykholt, Holar, Hallorasta-

37

dur. These are generally comfortable with good food. Prices from 10 kr. a day at Laugarvatn, the Gleneagles of Iceland, to 5 kr. inclusive. At Laugarvatn and Reykholt there are hot baths. There are also inns at Thingvellir and Geysir, and various other places, which are marked on the 4 miles to the inch maps. In the interior there are several saelihus or mountain huts, which again vary greatly in size and standard. These and camping sites are marked on Bruun's map. With regard to the other towns besides Reykjavik, there are three hotels in Akureyri, the nicest of which is the Gullfoss. In Isafjördur you can stay at the Salvation Army Hostel. Elsewhere difficulty and discomfort is to be expected. I recommend any single tourist who finds himself in Seydisfjördur to go to the old women's almshouses, where I was myself extremely comfortable.

Buses

There are excellent bus services to all parts of the island, except the North-West and the South-East, and the fares are very reasonable. There are, for example, four buses a week to Akureyri, a distance of about 300 kilometres, taking two days if you go by bus all the way, and one day if you take the motor ship *Laxfoss* to Borgarnes or Akranes. Single fare 30 kr. It is wise to book seats a day or two beforehand, and if staying on a bus route to telephone through to a previous stop. Where there are no official buses, there are often milk-cars which will take you very slowly but cheaply. Those who are car-sick will have, I'm afraid, a rough time. (The drivers are excellent.)

Horses and Guides

There are very few places in Iceland where it is pleasant to walk, and for long expeditions guides are absolutely necessary if you don't want to lose your horses or get drowned in a river. Besides, the farmers won't lend their horses without one. The price of a pony for a day varies from 3 kr. to 6 kr. in the fashionable places. The best ponies come from Skargafjördur in the North. For long journeys with a large party the price works out something like this:

Riding pony, 4 kr. per day—1 kr. for riding saddle   5 kr.
Pack pony,   3 kr. per day—2 kr. for pack saddle   5 kr.
Spare ponies, 3 kr. per day each   3 kr.
1st Guide per day   15 kr.
2nd Guide per day   10 kr.

For a party of seven plus two guides we needed seventeen horses, nine riding, five pack, and three spare.

I am told that some guides object to hobbling the horses at night. Ours hobbled them, but another party which did not take this precaution lost a whole day and one pony. On some expeditions fodder has to be carried.

Language

It is not to be expected that all the farmers will speak English, but a great many do speak a little, and an English-speaking guide can always be found, if you want one. German is also useful. There is a phrase-book for those who find that kind of thing any use, and for the conscientious there is Zoëga's *English-Icelandic Dictionary* (expensive and full of non-existent English words), and Snaebjorn Jonsson's *Primer of Modern Icelandic*.

Food.

In the larger hotels in Reykjavik you will of course get ordinary European food, but in the farms you will only get what there is, which is on the whole rather peculiar.

Breakfast: (9.0 a.m.). If you stay in a farm this will be brought to you in bed. Coffee, bread and cheese, and small cakes. Coffee, which is drunk all through the day—I must

39

have drunk about 1,500 cups in three months—is generally good. There is white bread, brown bread, rock-hard but quite edible, and unleavened rye bread like cake. The ordinary cheese is like a strong Dutch and good. There is also a brown sweet cheese, like the Norwegian. I don't like cakes so I never ate any, but other people say they are good.

Lunch and Dinner: (12 noon and 7 p.m.). If you are staying anywhere, lunch is the chief meal, but farmers are always willing to give you a chief meal at any time of the day or night that you care. (I once had supper at 11 p.m.)

Soups: Many of these are sweet and very unfortunate. I remember three with particular horror, one of sweet milk and hard macaroni, one tasting of hot marzipan, and one of scented hair oil. (But there is a good sweet soup, raspberry coloured, made of bilberry. L. M.)

Fish: Dried fish is a staple food in Iceland. This should be shredded with the fingers and eaten with butter. It varies in toughness. The tougher kind tastes like toe-nails, and the softer kind like the skin off the soles of one's feet.

In districts where salmon are caught, or round the coast, you get excellent fish, the grilled salmon particularly.

Meat: This is practically confined to mutton in various forms. The Danes have influenced Icelandic cooking, and to no advantage. Meat is liable to be served up in glutinous and half-cold lumps, covered with tasteless gravy. At the poorer farms you will only get Hángikyrl, *i.e.* smoked mutton. This is comparatively harmless when cold as it only tastes like soot, but it would take a very hungry man indeed to eat it hot.

Vegetables: Apart from potatoes, these, in the earlier part of the summer are conspicuous by their absence. Later, however, there are radishes, turnips, carrots, and lettuce in sweet milk. Newish potatoes begin to appear about the end of August. Boiled potatoes are eaten with melted butter, but beware of the browned potatoes, as they are coated in sugar, another Danish barbarism.

Fruit: None, except rhubarb and in the late summer excellent bilberries.

Cold Food: Following the Scandinavian custom, in the hotels, following the hot dish there are a number of dishes of cold meats and fishes eaten with bread and butter. Most of these are good, particularly the pickled herring. Smoked salmon in my opinion is an overrated dish, but it is common for those who appreciate it.

Sweets: The standard sweet is skyr, a cross between Devonshire cream and a cream cheese, which is eaten with sugar and cream. It is very filling but most people like it very much. It is not advisable, however, to take coffee and skyr together just before riding, as it gives you diarrhoea.

Tea: (4 p.m.). Coffee, cakes, and if you are lucky, pancakes with cream. These are wafer-thick and extremely good. Coffee and cake are also often brought you in the evening, about 10 p.m. Those who like tea or cocoa should bring it with them and supervise the making of it themselves.

Food for Expeditions

Bread, butter, cheese and coffee are safe to buy in Iceland. Those who can eat them will find the smoked mutton and dried fish travel well. There is also an excellent tinned and cooked mutton to be bought which is very useful. All chocolate or sweets should be bought in England.

Drink

Apart from coffee and milk and water, there is little to be said for the drink in Iceland, which is just recovering from Prohibition. In Reykjavik you can get drinks at the Borg if you can pay for them. A whisky and soda (Irish whisky is unobtainable) costs 2.25 kr.; and a glass of respectable sherry 1.45 kr. There are also government shops in various places where you can buy bottles furtively over the counter. They close at noon. A bottle of brown sherry cost me 9.50 kr. and a bottle of Spanish brandy (the only brandy they had) 6.50 kr. The beer is weak and nasty, and the lemonade unspeakable.

Illicit brandy can sometimes be got, and is sometimes insistently offered by friendly farmers, but it is deadly.

Oddities

For the curious there are two Icelandic foods which should certainly be tried. One is Hákarl, which is half-dry, half-rotten shark. This is white inside with a prickly horn rind outside, as tough as an old boot. Owing to the smell it has to be eaten out of doors. It is shaved off with a knife and eaten with brandy. It tastes more like boot-polish than anything else I can think of. The other is Reyngi. This is the tail of the whale, which is pickled in sour milk for a year or so. If you intend to try it, do not visit a whaling station first. Incidentally, talking about pickling in sour milk, the Icelanders also do this to sheeps' udders, and the result is surprisingly very nice.

Tobacco

There is a fairly wide range of choice both of cigarettes and pipe tobaccos in Reykjavik, but in the country nothing is obtainable but Commanders, an English cigarette which seems to be manufactured solely for export to Iceland.

Photography

Agfa and Kodak films can be got in Reykjavik, and sometimes in other towns, but it is not worth risking getting them elsewhere. You can get films developed in Reykjavik, but if you are particular about the results it is better to bring them home. As a complete tyro, it is presumptuous of me to give advice, but from my experience and that of others more competent than I, I think that in Iceland, even if you are using a meter, there is a tendency to over-expose.

Where to go

This of course depends on the individual. Those with special tastes like fishing, ornithology, or geology will know for themselves. Most tourists will presumably want to see Thingvellir and Geysir, but they should not miss Grylla, a small geyser in the South which spouts every two hours. The hearty will want to go to the interior, and a journey round the Langjökull is probably as good as any. Time from 7 to 9 days. Inclusive price for a largish party, a little over £12 a head. For the tough there is Vatnajökull or Askja. For those who like riding for its own sake, it is a little difficult to find large stretches of open flat country. Perhaps the delta of the Markaflot and the Thorsá in the South is the best, though they may find difficulty in getting really good horses there. For those who want to stay quietly in one place there are a number of places. Personally I should recommend either Reykholt in the West or Egilsstadur or Hallorastadur in the East.

If I had a fortnight to spend myself I should go to the North-West, as I think it both the most beautiful and the least visited part of Iceland. You come to Isafjördur by the Icelandic boats from Reykjavik, and move about either by horses or motor-boat. Anyone who does think of going there should get in touch with the British Vice-consul at Isafjördur, Mr. Joachimsson, who is extremely kind and efficient.

For Motorists

Those who regard motoring as a convenient means of seeing places and not as an end in itself, and who like a holiday off the beaten track, might do worse than turn their attention towards Iceland. There has been a great deal of road-building since the war and from the map at the end of this book it will be seen that most of the island, except the north-west peninsula, the tract of glacier rivers south-east of the Vatnajökull, and the desert in the centre, can be now reached by car, and indeed along most of the roads there are already bus services. I travelled about largely by bus and am convinced that it is one of the best ways of seeing the country, though I should have preferred being able to stop when and where I liked, and the hire of private cars is very expensive. A road in Iceland, of course, is not always what one knows in England by that name. The roads to Thingvellir and Laugarvatn, those in Borgafirth, and indeed most of the road from Borgarnes to Akureyri, are fairly good third-class English roads.

The road from Husavik to Grimsstadur, on the other hand, consists of two ruts, along which the maximum speed is about 8 kilometres per hour, and the Thingvellir hill on the Thingvellir-Laugarvatn road is barely negotiable. Still cars do go along all these roads without mishap. I am told that they very rarely break a back-axle as they cannot go fast enough to do that, but that spare springs should always be carried. The commonest cars in Iceland are large American ones, mainly Chevrolets, but smaller-powered cars if strongly built are quite adequate, as the majority of the gradients, other than short dips over streams, are less than you would expect in a mountainous country. A high ground clearance is, however, essential. On the better roads the wheel tracks are sunk in loose grit, leaving a raised middle section for horses, and care is needed at higher speeds to avoid skidding. All bridges and nearly all roads are single, and passing another car means stopping.

The Icelanders are all sick in the buses, but a driver told me he had never known an Englishman to be. Practically every farm will put tourists up, and, though of course the accommodation is often limited and primitive, the farmers make every effort to do their best for one. Cars can always be left without anxiety as to their safety or the safety of things left in them, so that it is perfectly possible to combine motoring expeditions with trips on horses to places where motors cannot go. I had no personal experiences of garages, but I am told that there are good ones in Reykjavik and Akureyri. Elsewhere, of course, the driver must do his own repairs. It is unnecessary to carry spare petrol as the maximum distance between pumps is 58 kilometres, but running out of petrol means probably a long walk to the next station and a long ride back. The petrol is B.P. or Shell, price 32 öre per litre (about 1s. 5d. a gallon).

The Icelandic Shipping Company is prepared to ship cars from Hull or Leith. If there are five passengers, the fifth travels free. If there are four, there is no extra charge and so on. On arrival in Iceland, particulars about roads and regulations can be obtained from the Stat-Tourist bureau in Reykjavik, near the harbour. An international driving licence is sufficient, and there is no car tax. Outside the towns there is no speed limit, but an average of 30 kilometres an hour is about as much as one can generally manage. Drive on the left.

BIBLIOGRAPHY

General Information
Icelandic Year-Book, *Iceland*, 1930.
Stefan Stefansson: *Iceland for Tourists.*

For Tourists

Language
Snaebjorn Jonsson: *A Primer of Modern Icelandic.*
Zoëga: *Ensk-Islenzk Ordabok; Islenzk-Ensk Ordabok.*

History and Literature
Knut Gjerset: *History of Iceland.*
W. P. Ker: *Epic and Romance; The Dark Ages; Collected Essays.*
Dame Philpot: *Edda and Saga.*
W. G. Craigie: *The Icelandic Sagas.*
Professor G. V. Gordon: *An Introduction to Old Norse; Romance in Iceland.*
F. L. Lucas: *Decline and Fall of the Romantic Tradition.*

Travel
See Bibliography to Chapter VI.

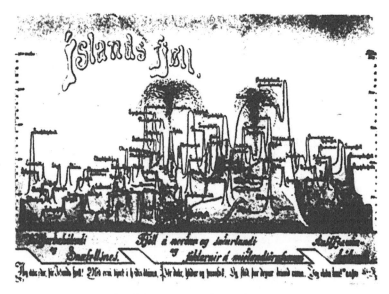

The Mountains of Iceland

Chapter V

Letter to Lord Byron

PART II

————◆◆◆————

I'm writing this in pencil on my knee,
        Using my other hand to stop me yawning,
Upon a primitive, unsheltered quay
        In the small hours of a Wednesday morning.
        I cannot add the summer day is dawning;
In Seythisfjördur every schoolboy knows
That daylight in the summer never goes.

To get to sleep in latitudes called upper
        Is difficult at first for Englishmen.
It's like being sent to bed before your supper
        For playing darts with father's fountain-pen,
        Or like returning after orgies, when
Your breath's like luggage and you realise
You've been more confidential than was wise.

I've done my duty, taken many notes
        Upon the almost total lack of greenery,
The roads, the illegitimates, the goats:
        To use a rhyme of yours, there's handsome scenery
        But little agricultural machinery;
And with the help of Sunlight Soap the Geysir
Affords to visitors le plus grand plaisir.

47

The North, though, never was your cup of tea;
    'Moral' you thought it so you kept away.
And what I'm sure you're wanting now from me
    Is news about the England of the day,
    What sort of things La Jeunesse do and say.
Is Brighton still as proud of her pavilion,
And is it safe for girls to travel pillion?

I'll clear my throat and take a Rover's breath
    And skip a century of hope and sin—
For far too much has happened since your death.
    Crying went out and the cold bath came in,
    With drains, bananas, bicycles, and tin,
And Europe saw from Ireland to Albania
The Gothic revival and the Railway Mania.

We're entering now the Eotechnic Phase
    Thanks to the Grid and all those new alloys;
That is, at least, what Lewis Mumford says.
    A world of Aertex underwear for boys,
    Huge plate-glass windows, walls absorbing noise,
Where the smoke nuisance is utterly abated
And all the furniture is chromium-plated.

Well, you might think so if you went to Surrey
    And stayed for week-ends with the well to do,
Your car too fast, too personal your worry
    To look too closely at the wheeling view.
    But in the north it simply isn't true.
To those who live in Warrington or Wigan,
It's not a white lie, it's a whacking big 'un.

There on the old historic battlefield,
    The cold ferocity of human wills,
The scars of struggle are as yet unhealed;
    Slattern the tenements on sombre hills,
    And gaunt in valleys the square-windowed mills

48

That, since the Georgian house, in my conjecture
Remain our finest native architecture.

On economic, health, or moral grounds
    It hasn't got the least excuse to show;
No more than chamber pots or otter hounds:
    But let me say before it has to go,
    It's the most lovely country that I know;
Clearer than Scafell Pike, my heart has stamped on
The view from Birmingham to Wolverhampton.

Long, long ago, when I was only four,
    Going towards my grandmother, the line
Passed through a coal-field. From the corridor
    I watched it pass with envy, thought 'How fine!
    Oh how I wish that situation mine.'
Tramlines and slagheaps, pieces of machinery,
That was, and still is, my ideal scenery.

Hail to the New World! Hail to those who'll love
    Its antiseptic objects, feel at home.
Lovers will gaze at an electric stove,
    Another poésie de départ come
    Centred round bus-stops or the aerodrome.
But give me still, to stir imagination
The chiaroscuro of the railway station.

Preserve me from the Shape of Things to Be;
   The high-grade posters at the public meeting,
The influence of Art on Industry,
    The cinemas with perfect taste in seating;
    Preserve me, above all, from central heating.
It may be D. H. Lawrence hocus-pocus,
But I prefer a room that's got a focus.

But you want facts, not sighs. I'll do my best
    To give a few; you can't expect them all.
49

To start with, on the whole we're better dressed;
>   For chic the difference to-day is small
>   Of barmaid from my lady at the Hall.
It's sad to spoil this democratic vision
With millions suffering from malnutrition.

Again, our age is highly educated;
>   There is no lie our children cannot read,
And as MacDonald might so well have stated
>   We're growing up and up and up indeed.
>   Advertisements can teach us all we need;
And death is better, as the millions know,
Than dandruff, night-starvation, or B.O.

We've always had a penchant for field sports,
>   But what do you think has grown up in our towns?
A passion for the open air and shorts;
>   The sun is one of our emotive nouns.
>   Go down by chara' to the Sussex Downs,
Watch the manœuvres of the week-end hikers
Massed on parade with Kodaks or with Leicas.

These movements signify our age-long rule
>   Of insularity has lost its powers;
The cult of salads and the swimming pool
>   Comes from a climate sunnier than ours,
>   And lands which never heard of licensed hours.
The south of England before very long
Will look no different from the Continong.

You lived and moved among the best society
>   And so could introduce your hero to it
Without the slightest tremor of anxiety;
>   Because he was your hero and you knew it,
>   He'd know instinctively what's done, and do it.
He'd find our day more difficult than yours
For Industry has mixed the social drawers.

We've grown, you see, a lot more democratic,
    And Fortune's ladder is for all to climb;
Carnegie on this point was most emphatic.
    A humble grandfather is not a crime,
    At least, if father made enough in time!
To-day, thank God, we've got no snobbish feeling
Against the more efficient modes of stealing.

The porter at the Carlton is my brother,
    He'll wish me a good evening if I pay,
For tips and men are equal to each other.
    I'm sure that *Vogue* would be the first to say
    Que le Beau Monde is socialist to-day;
And many a bandit, not so gently born
Kills vermin every winter with the Quorn.

Adventurers, though, must take things as they find them
    And look for pickings where the pickings are.
The drives of love and hunger are behind them,
    They can't afford to be particular:
    And those who like good cooking and a car,
A certain kind of costume or of face,
Must seek them in a certain kind of place.

Don Juan was a mixer and no doubt
    Would find this century as good as any
For getting hostesses to ask him out,
    And mistresses that need not cost a penny.
    Indeed our ways to waste time are so many,
Thanks to technology, a list of these
Would make a longer book than *Ulysses*.

Yes, in the smart set he would know his way
    By second nature with no tips from me.
Tennis and Golf have come in since your day;
    But those who are as good at games as he
    Acquire the back-hand quite instinctively,

51

Take to the steel-shaft and hole out in one,
Master the books of Ely Culbertson.

I see his face in every magazine.
    'Don Juan at lunch with one of Cochran's ladies.'
'Don Juan with his red setter May MacQueen.'
      'Don Juan, who's just been wintering in Cadiz,
      Caught at the wheel of his maroon Mercedes.'
'Don Juan at Croydon Aerodrome.' 'Don Juan
Snapped in the paddock with the Agha Khan.'

But if in highbrow circles he would sally
    It's just as well to warn him there's no stain on
Picasso, all-in-wrestling, or the Ballet.
    Sibelius is the man. To get a pain on
    Listening to Elgar is a sine qua non.
A second-hand acquaintance of Pareto's
Ranks higher than an intimate of Plato's.

The vogue for Black Mass and the cult of devils
    Has sunk. The Good, the Beautiful, the True
Still fluctuate about the lower levels.
    Joyces are firm and there there's nothing new.
    Eliots have hardened just a point or two.
Hopkins are brisk, thanks to some recent boosts.
There's been some further weakening in Prousts.

I'm saying this to tell you who's the rage,
    And not to loose a sneer from my interior.
Because there's snobbery in every age,
    Because some names are loved by the superior,
    It does not follow they're the least inferior:
For all I know the Beatific Vision's
On view at all Surrealist Exhibitions.

Now for the spirit of the people. Here
    I know I'm treading on more dangerous ground:

I know they're many changes in the air,
 But know my data too slight to be sound.
 I know, too, I'm inviting the renowned
Retort of all who love the Status Quo:
'You can't change human nature, don't you know!'

We've still, it's true, the same shape and appearance,
 We haven't changed the way that kissing's done;
The average man still hates all interference,
 Is just as proud still of his new-born son:
 Still, like a hen, he likes his private run,
Scratches for self-esteem, and slyly pecks
A good deal in the neighbourhood of sex.

But he's another man in many ways:
 Ask the cartoonist first, for he knows best.
Where is the John Bull of the good old days,
 The swaggering bully with the clumsy jest?
 His meaty neck has long been laid to rest,
His acres of self-confidence for sale;
He passed away at Ypres and Passchendaele.

Turn to the work of Disney or of Strube;
 There stands our hero in his threadbare seams;
The bowler hat who straphangs in the tube,
 And kicks the tyrant only in his dreams,
 Trading on pathos, dreading all extremes;
The little Mickey with the hidden grudge;
Which is the better, I leave you to judge.

Begot on Hire-Purchase by Insurance,
 Forms at his christening worshipped and adored;
A season ticket schooled him in endurance,
 A tax collector and a waterboard
 Admonished him. In boyhood he was awed
By a matric, and complex apparatuses
Keep his heart conscious of Divine Afflatuses.

'I am like you', he says, 'and you, and you,
 I love my life, I love the home-fires, have
To keep them burning. Heroes never do.
 Heroes are sent by ogres to the grave.
 I may not be courageous, but I save.
I am the one who somehow turns the corner,
I may perhaps be fortunate Jack Horner.

I am the ogre's private secretary;
 I've felt his stature and his powers, learned
To give his ogreship the raspberry
 Only when his gigantic back is turned.
 One day, who knows, I'll do as I have yearned.
The short man, all his fingers on the door,
With repartee shall send him to the floor.'

One day, which day? O any other day,
 But not to-day. The ogre knows his man.
To kill the ogre that would take away
 The fear in which his happy dreams began,
 And with his life he'll guard dreams while he can.
Those who would really kill his dream's contentment
He hates with real implacable resentment.

He dreads the ogre, but he dreads yet more
 Those who conceivably might set him free,
Those the cartoonist has no time to draw.
 Without his bondage he'd be all at sea;
 The ogre need but shout 'Security',
To make this man, so loveable, so mild,
As madly cruel as a frightened child.

Byron, thou should'st be living at this hour!
 What would you do, I wonder, if you were?
Britannia's lost prestige and cash and power,
 Her middle classes show some wear and tear,
 We've learned to bomb each other from the air;

I can't imagine what the Duke of Wellington
Would say about the music of Duke Ellington.

Suggestions have been made that the Teutonic
 Führer-Prinzip would have appealed to you
As being the true heir to the Byronic—
 In keeping with your social status too
 (It has its English converts, fit and few),
That you would, hearing honest Oswald's call,
Be gleichgeschaltet in the Albert Hall.

'Lord Byron at the head of his storm-troopers!'
 Nothing, says science, is impossible:
The Pope may quit to join the Oxford Groupers,
 Nuffield may leave one farthing in his Will,
 There may be someone who trusts Baldwin still,
Someone may think that Empire wines are nice,
There may be people who hear Tauber twice.

You liked to be the centre of attention,
 The gay Prince Charming of the fairy story,
Who tamed the Dragon by his intervention.
 In modern warfare though it's just as gory,
 There isn't any individual glory;
The Prince must be anonymous, observant,
A kind of lab-boy, or a civil servant.

You never were an Isolationist;
 Injustice you had always hatred for,
And we can hardly blame you, if you missed
 Injustice just outside your lordship's door:
 Nearer than Greece were cotton and the poor.
To-day you might have seen them, might indeed
Have walked in the United Front with Gide,

Against the ogre, dragon, what you will;
 His many shapes and names all turn us pale,

Letter to Lord Byron

For he's immortal, and to-day he still
    Swinges the horror of his scaly tail.
    Sometimes he seems to sleep, but will not fail
In every age to rear up to defend
Each dying force of history to the end.

Milton beheld him on the English throne,
    And Bunyan sitting in the Papal chair;
The hermits fought him in their caves alone,
    At the first Empire he was also there,
    Dangling his Pax Romana in the air:
He comes in dreams at puberty to man,
To scare him back to childhood if he can.

Banker or landlord, booking-clerk or Pope,
    Whenever he's lost faith in choice and thought,
When a man sees the future without hope,
    Whenever he endorses Hobbes' report
    'The life of man is nasty, brutish, short',
The dragon rises from his garden border
And promises to set up law and order.

He that in Athens murdered Socrates,
    And Plato then seduced, prepares to make
A desolation and to call it peace
    To-day for dying magnates, for the sake
    Of generals who can scarcely keep awake,
And for that doughy mass in great and small
That doesn't want to stir itself at all.

Forgive me for inflicting all this on you,
    For asking you to hold the baby for us;
It's easy to forget that where you've gone, you
    May only want to chat with Set and Horus,
    Bored to extinction with our earthly chorus:
Perhaps it sounds to you like a trunk-call,
Urgent, it seems, but quite inaudible.

Yet though the choice of what is to be done
    Remains with the alive, the rigid nation
Is supple still within the breathing one;
    Its sentinels yet keep their sleepless station,
    And every man in every generation,
Tossing in his dilemma on his bed,
Cries to the shadows of the noble dead.

We're out at sea now, and I wish we weren't;
    The sea is rough, I don't care if it's blue;
I'd like to have a quick one, but I daren't.
    And I must interrupt this screed to you,
    For I've some other little jobs to do;
I must write home or mother will be vexed,
So this must be continued in our next.

END OF PART II

Chapter VI

Sheaves from Sagaland

An Anthology of Icelandic Travel addressed to John Betjeman, Esq.

Iceland is real

'Iceland is not a myth; it is a solid portion of the earth's surface.'—Pliny Miles.

Where is Iceland?

'I made several observations with an excellent Paris Quadrant, and ascertained the elevation of the pole by means of a lunar eclipse which happened in December, 1750. By a telescope accurately furnished with a micrometer, I took the exact latitude of the island, and having determined it in a nicer manner than it ever was before, found that Iceland lies almost four degrees more to the east than it has hitherto been computed.'—Horrebow.

What does Iceland look like?

'The map of Iceland has been sometimes drawn by schoolboys as an eider duck, quacking with wide-opened beak.'—Collingwood.

Impressions of a Viking

'To that place of fish may I never come in my old age.' —Ketil Flatnose.

58

Impressions of a Poet
  'A gallows of slush.'—A Tenth Century Scald.

Impressions of the Middle Ages
            'To speak of Iceland is little need;
            Save of stockfish.'—Hakluyt.

Impressions of an Archbishop
  'On our arrival in Iceland we directly saw a prospect before us which, though not pleasing, was uncommon and
surprising, and our eyes, accustomed to behold the pleasing coasts of England, now saw nothing but the vestiges
of the operation of a fire, Heaven knows how ancient.'
—Van Troil.

Iceland is German
  'Für uns Island ist das Land.'—An unknown Nazi.

Concerning the Scenery
  'Alone in Iceland you are alone indeed and the home-
less, undisturbed wilderness gives something of its awful
calm to the spirit. It was like listening to noble music, yet
perplexed and difficult to follow. If the Italian landscape
is like Mozart; if in Switzerland the sublimity and sweet-
ness correspond in art to Beethoven; then we may take
Iceland as the type of nature of the music of the moderns
—say Schumann at his oddest and wildest.'—Miss Oswald.

Concerning the Mountains
  'This author says that the mountains are nothing but
sand and stone.'—Horrebow.

Concerning the uses of Volcanoes
  'Surely were it possible for those thoughtless and in-
sensible beings whose minds seem impervious to every
finer feeling to be suddenly transported to this burning
region and placed within view of the tremendous opera-
tions of the vomiting pool, the sight could not but arouse

59

them from their lethargic stupor, and by superinducing habits of serious reflection might be attended with the happiest consequences, both to themselves and all within the sphere of their influence.'—Henderson.

Concerning the Vegetation

'Nowhere a single tree appears which might afford shelter to friendship and innocence.'—Van Troil.

Concerning the Climate

'Those who gave an account that it was so hot that they were obliged to go almost naked, had that day, I suppose, great quantities of fish to weigh out, and send aboard their respective ships.'—Horrebow.

Concerning the Wild Life

'It is commonly reported that the noise and bellowing of these seabulls and seacows makes the cows ashore run mad. But none here ever saw any of these supposed animals, or noticed the bad effects of their bellowing.'
—*Ibid.*

Concerning the Insect Life

'McKenzie found a coccinella near the Geysir: and Madame Ida Pfeiffer secured two wild bees which she carried off in spirits of wine.'—Burton.

Concerning the Capital

'Reykjavik is, unquestionably, the worst place in which to spend the winter in Iceland. The tone of society is the lowest that can well be imagined. . . . It not only presents a lamentable blank to the view of the religious observer, but is totally devoid of every source of intellectual gratification.'—Henderson.

The Immortal Bard proves that nothing escapes him

'Pish for thee, Iceland dog. Thou prick-eared cur of Iceland.'—Shakespeare: *Henry IV.*

The Icelanders are human

'They are not so robust and hardy that nothing can hurt them; for they are human beings and experience the sensations common to mankind.'—Horrebow.

Concerning their hair

'The hair which belongs to the class Lissotriches, subdivision Euplokamo, seldom shows the darker shades of brown. The colour ranges from carroty red to turnip yellow, from barley-sugar to the blond-cendré so expensive in the civilised markets. We find all the gradations of Parisian art here natural; the corn golden, the blonde fulvide, the incandescent (carroty), the florescent or sulphur-hued, the beurre frais, the fulvastre or lion's mane, and the rubide or mahogany, Raphael's favourite tint.'—Burton.

Concerning their eyes

'A very characteristic feature of the race is the eye, dure and cold as a pebble—the mesmerist would despair at the first sight.'—*Ibid.*

Concerning their mouths

'The oral region is often coarse and unpleasant.'—*Ibid.*

Concerning their temperament

'The Icelander's temperament is nervoso-lymphatic and at best nervoso-sanguineous.'—*Ibid.*

Concerning their appearance

'The Icelanders are of a good, honest disposition, but they are at the same time so serious and sullen that I hardly remember to have seen any of them laugh.'—Van Troil.

Concerning their character

'This poor but highly respectable people.'—McKenzie.

Concerning their sensibility

'The Icelanders in general are civil and well-disposed, but they are said not to feel strongly.'—Barrow.

No nonsense about the Icelanders

'Practical men in Iceland vigorously deny the existence of the Gulf Stream.'—Burton.

Disadvantages of the North Pole

'It is possible the Icelanders are not now as barbarous as formerly though it may rationally be supposed that a nation living so near the North Pole may not be so refined and polished as some others, especially among the vulgar sort, for people of fashion ought to be exempted from this rule (less or more) in most places.'—Tremarec.

Concerning their courage

'They are far from being a dastardly race as some authors have represented them; for it is well-known that they made some figure in a military life, and have been raised to the command of a fortress.'—Horrebow.

Concerning their morals

' "Happy the nations of the moral North" wrote Byron some years since. Without imagining that they are worse than their neighbours I fancy it is very much like the ideal morality of the so-termed middle-classes, which has been of late so ruthlessly shattered by Sir Cresswell Cresswell.' —Forbes.

Concerning their food

'It cannot afford any great pleasure to examine the manner in which the Icelanders prepare their food.'—Van Troil.

Concerning their butter

'Their butter looks very well and I could have ate it for the looks, if my nose did not tell me that it could not taste well. Mr. Anderson says their butter looks green, black and of all colours.'—Horrebow.

Concerning Hákarl
'This had so disagreeable a taste that the small quantity we took of it drove us from the table long before our intention.'—Van Troil.

Eat more fish
'Ichthyophagy and idleness must do much to counterbalance the sun-clad power of chastity.'—Burton.

Concerning their habits
'If I attempted to describe some of their nauseous habits, I might fill volumes.'—Pfeiffer.

A young lady's opinion
'The Icelanders have no idea of out-of-doors amenity.' —Miss Oswald.

Concerning their dress
'The dress of the women is not calculated to show the person to advantage.'—McKenzie.

Concerning their baths
'The inhabitants do not bathe in them here merely for their health, but they are likewise the occasion for a scene of gallantry. Poverty prevents here the lover from making presents to his fair one, and Nature presents no flowers of which elsewhere garlands are made: 'tis therefore customary that instead of all this the swain perfectly cleanses one of these baths which is afterwards honoured by the visit of his bride.'—Van Troil.

Concerning their kissing
'I have sometimes fancied, when they took their faces apart, that I could hear a slight clicking sound; but this might be imagination.'—Howell.

Concerning their laundry

'They wash their things tolerably well, though I must suppose, not to the liking of all persons.'—Horrebow.

Concerning their music

'I heard a voice in the farm singing an Icelandic song. At a distance it resembled the humming of bees.'—Pfeiffer.

Concerning their dancing

'They have no idea of dancing, though sometimes the merchants at the factories for their diversion will get a fiddle and make them dance, in which they succeed no better than by hopping and jumping about.'—Horrebow.

Concerning their sculpture

'Thorwaldson, the son of an Icelander, dwelling on the classic ground of Rome, is at the present moment second only to Canova among the statuaries of Europe.'—McKenzie.

Concerning their chessmen

'There is not a peasant in the country but what has a set, which they make out of fishbones. The whole difference betwixt theirs and ours being that our fools stand for their bishops because they say the clergyman ought to be near the King's person. Their rooks represent little captains whom the Icelandic scholars call their Centuriones. They are represented with swords at their sides, with bloated cheeks, as if they were blowing the horns they hold in both their hands.'—Tremarec.

Good news for the Geography Mistress

'The search for this useful lichen forms the annual holiday of Icelandic girlhood.'—Howell.

Bad news for the Watch Committee

'The Elder Edda may be searched through and through and there will not be found a single nude myth, not an

impersonation of any kind that can be considered an out-
rage upon virtue or a violation of the laws of propriety.'
—Anderson.

Concerning their literary criticism

'In all departments of literature, there is a strong disposition among the Icelanders to critical severity. A
curious instance of this kind occurred about a hundred
years ago when an unfortunate man was publicly whipped
as a punishment for the errors he had committed in a
translation of the book of Genesis.'—McKenzie.

Concerning their lack of education

'It is not uncommon in Iceland for people of all ranks,
ages and sexes to sleep in the same apartment. Their no-
tions of decency are unavoidably not very refined; but we
had sufficient proof that the instances of this which we
witnessed proceeded from ignorance, and expressed nothing but perfect innocence.'—*Ibid.*

Concerning their high-grade living

'Publications connected with practical morality are very
common in Iceland, and several excellent books of this kind
have lately appeared in the island, adapted chiefly to the use
of farmers or those of the middle-classes; in which moral
instruction is judiciously blended with amusing information in various branches of knowledge. The most valuable
of these writings is a work called *Evening Hours*.'—*Ibid.*

Concerning their religion

'The influence of the Lutheran Church is practically
universal, the Nonconformists of the island numbering
probably but one or two of the Brethren, and a single
Swedenborgian.'—Howell.

Plato in the North

'Some of the clergy of the new school, instead of drawing
the matter of their sermons from the Scriptures, gather it

from the writings of heathen philosophers, and the morality found in these authors, which at the best is but dry and insipid, absolutely freezes when transported to Iceland.'—Henderson.

The Scarlet Woman in Iceland

'An American organ leads the singing, which is slow but none the less devotional, and thoroughly Congregational. A gaudy red and yellow robe which the pastor wears during a portion of the liturgy is evidently a survival of the Romanist days. His black gown and white ruff are less obtrusive and more in keeping with a Christian service.' —Howell.

Concerning their behaviour in Church

'Most of the congregation sat with their faces turned towards the altar, but the rule had its exceptions.'— Pfeiffer.

Concerning the literary taste of the Clergy

'Assessor Grondal also composed several poetical satires in which, according to the information of the Bishop, there is much successful ridicule.'—McKenzie.

Concerning the isolation of real Christians in Iceland

'The greater number of these individuals are, in all probability, known only to God, having little intercourse with each other, and the situation may, not unfitly, be compared to that of the generality of real Christians in Scotland about thirty or forty years ago.'—Henderson.

A Problem for Missionaries

'A church was built in 984 by Thorvald Bodvarter and some persons received baptism, but others, though they had no objection to the Christian religion, could not be prevailed upon to suffer themselves to be baptised, as they pretended it would be indecent to go naked into the water, like little boys.'—Van Troil.

A use for Icelandic women

'As wives they would be efficient correctives to the fine drawn framework and the over-nervous diathesis of southern nations.'—Burton.

Tiddley om pom pom

'Die geistige Aufgeschlossenheit und rasche Aufnahme-fähigkeit der Isländischen Frau hat in der Stadt in den letzen zehn Jahren einer Typus hervorgebracht, der die Eleganz und das künstliche Modespiel der Städtischen Festländerinnen noch zu überbieten trachtet. Das alles verfleucht jedoch wie ein dünner Spuk, wenn eine Islän-dische Frau einher schreitet in der Königlichen Festtracht ihres Landes und in Gewand und Haltung einer einzigen solchen Gestalt Tausendjähriges Isländertum in seiner menschlichen Stärke enthüllt.'—Prinz.

The longest word in Icelandic

Haestarjettarmalaflutunesmanskifstofustulkonutidyra-lykill—a latch-key belonging to a girl working in the office of a barrister.

PART III.—THE TOURIST

Iceland is safe

'An eruption very seldom happens, and even when it does, it occupies but a small tract of time. Travellers can-not therefore be much obstructed by it.'—Horrebow.

Reassurance to Girl Guides

'What! says someone, can ladies travel in Iceland? Cer-tainly, as witness the expeditions of Miss Oswald and Miss Adelia Gates.'—Howell.

A warning

'To be well received here it is necessary either to be rich or else to travel as a naturalist.'—Pfeiffer.

Why go there? A reason

'Well, Rector, you are partly right. I do like getting out
of the regions of respectability—pardon me—once in a
way. Hard fare, too, for a time is a fine alternative. Persi-
cos odi apparatus.'—Metcalfe.

Another reason

'The traveller enjoys for himself the most absolute immunity; he may be offered a seat in the Cabinet, or accused
of forgery, or portrayed in Vanity Fair,—he will know nothing about it till his return.'—Viscount Bryce.

The Voyage Out. A cautious simile

'Whales ahead—their spoky back fins revolving close
after each other in regular succession like the wheel of the
Great Eastern, if it has one.'—Metcalfe.

First sight of Iceland

'So I have seen Iceland at last. I awoke from a dream of
the Grange, which, by the way, was like some house at
Queen's Gate.'—William Morris.

Ditto

'We were delighted at seeing some new faces, in spite of
their nastiness and stench; and their grotesque appearance
afforded us much amusement.'—Hooker.

Character of a traveller

'Next I will introduce Mr. Darwin, a really celebrated
personage. He had written a learned book on Northern
Antiquities in recompense of which a Scandinavian poten-
tate created him a Knight of the second class of the Order
of the Walrus, the riband of which illustrious Order was
suspended across his brawny shoulders.'—Umbra.

Character of a light blue

'A man taking delight in museums and houses of assem-
bly, given to chemistry and the variations of European

politics, fond of statistics and well instructed in stuffed vermin.'—Anthony Trollope.

I was at B.N.C.

'It is very hard for a European, and perhaps especially hard for a graduate of one of the older English Universities to appreciate the squalid culture of these northern peoples.' —Annandale.

A French humanitarian

'Que les agranomes et les membres du club des Jockeys vantent les belles races de mérinos et les familles pur sang de chevaux anglais. Pour moi dusse-je faire vivre ceux qui n'ait jamais compati aux souffrances des animaux, j'avouerai que, dans mes excursions en Islande, j'ai souvent pressé entre mes mains, avec attendrissement, la tête de mon cheval.'—Marmier.

An unfavourable comparison

'The French author gives a life-like sketch of the difference between the sailors who man these ships. The Frenchman, working for the owner, landing at times, listless, idle, with a pocket as lean as his poor cadaverous face, hopeless, miserable to a degree. The Yankee, paddling his own canoe, pocketing all the gains, dashing ashore in his civilian dress, and flinging his dollars everywhere, drinking, roystering, catching the ponies, and scampering off, frightening the Icelander out of his wits.'—Howell.

Mr. X.

'I discovered a curious fact about Mr. X. which accounted for that gentleman's occasional readiness in making a quotation. Every night he wrapped himself in a large grey plaid of which he was very proud; it had been, he said, his companion in the mountains of Mexico. I now happened to examine some scarlet letters on the plaid and, to my amazement, discovered whole passages from Shake-

speare and other poets embroidered in red silk. In fact
Mr. X. slept in a book and could always refresh his memory
by studying when he woke.'—Umbra.

A poet's athletic feat

'Had that celebrated Pope whose Christian name was
Alexander believed that his immortal essay would have
been translated into Icelandic verse, by a native Icelander,
he would not have vaulted clear over the volcanic isle.'
—Miles.

Influence of the Gothic revival

'There was not one in our company who did not wish to
have his clothes a little singed for the sake of seeing Hekla
in a blaze.'—Van Troil.

An inarticulate Wordsworthian

'I wish it were in my power, Sir, to give you such a description of this place as it deserves, but I fear mine will
always remain inferior in point of expression. So much is
certain, at least, Nature never drew from anyone a more
cheerful homage to her Great Creator than I here paid
Him.'—*Ibid.*

Trials of a geologist

'Some of the pieces I handed to Arni to carry, who took
them very reluctantly; the bulk, however, were by degrees
thrown away, each succeeding rest seeing one or more of
the specimens abandoned which at the rest preceding I had
determined to preserve; greatly to the amusement of H.,
who is not disposed to subject himself to the least incon-
venience for the cause of science.'—W. G. Locke.

Trials of an author

'For a few minutes they remained quiet; then they began to whisper one to another, "She writes. She writes." '
—Pfeiffer.

A fast Victorian

'There was no alternative; I must either turn back or mount as a man. Keeping my brother at my side, and bidding the rest ride forward, I made him shorten the stirrups and hold the saddle, and after sundry attempts succeeded in landing myself man fashion on the animal's back. The position felt very odd at first, and I was also somewhat uncomfortable at my attitude, but on Vaughan's assuring me there was no cause for my uneasiness, and arranging my dress so that it fell in folds on either side, I decided to give the experiment a fair trial. Perhaps my boldness may rather surprise my readers.'—Mrs. Alice Tweedie.

Acumen of a religious observer

'Having gained some knowledge of the Icelandic beforehand, I could easily collect the scope and substance of his discourse, and, from its general tenor, do not hesitate to pronounce it strictly Evangelical.'—Henderson.

Inability of a Bishop to draw the line

'Here we saw the bishop himself countenancing vice in its worst shape, and appearing perfectly familiar with persons who, he must have known, bore the worst characters.' —McKenzie.

Privations of a traveller

'As long as I remained in Iceland I was compelled to give up my German system of diet.'—Pfeiffer.

An exchange of courtesies

'I plucked a flower, and speedily they brought a bunch. I touched a stone and half a dozen were at once forthcoming. However, I let them see that this was quite unnecessary.'—Howell.

The translator of the Arabian Nights gets the raspberry

'Among the gentler sex a soft look is uncommonly rare, and the aspect ranges from a stony stare to a

sharp glance rendered fiercer by the habitual frown.'—
Burton.

A psychological observation

'A certain feeling of discomfort always attached to the
fact of sleeping in a church alone in the midst of a grave-
yard.'—Pfeiffer.

Curious behaviour of a Scotch baronet

'We instantly left our guides and the horses to manage
matters as they could; and rushing over slags, lava, and
mud, fell upon the snow like wild beasts upon their prey.
My enjoyment was excessive; and the very recollection of
it is so gratifying that I must be excused for recording a
circumstance of so little importance.'—McKenzie.

Art without malice

'The clergyman had a large family and McDiarmed
good-naturedly took a blooming little maiden of six or
seven years a ride on his pony; while Lord Lodbrog drew a
very accurate sketch of his home and church. It was really
very well done and when pinned up against the wall of the
sitting-room had a smart appearance.'—Umbra.

Hear, Hear!

'Let's go home. We can't camp in this beastly place.
— What is he saying?
— I'm not going to camp here.
— You must. All Englishmen do.
— Blast all Englishmen.'—William Morris.

Moral drawn from a Geysir

'While the jets were rushing up towards Heaven with
the velocity of an arrow my mind was forcibly borne along
with them to the contemplation of the Great and Omni-
potent JEHOVAH in comparison with whom these and all
the wonders scattered over the whole immensity of existence dwindle into absolute insignificance; whose almighty

commands spake the universe into being; and at whose sovereign fiat the whole fabric might be reduced, in an instant, to its original nothing.'—Henderson.

Rudeness shown to the same Geysir

'Darwin profanely called the Geysir an old brute.'—Umbra.

Spread of Nazi Doctrines among the Icelandic ponies

'Famous scientists, doctors, politicians, and writers, mounted her and rode for a wonderful week's tour. Richer in experience, strengthened and refreshed by Nature, ready for a new struggle with the arch-fiend culture, they went home and gave lectures.'—Fleuron.

PART IV.—HOME AGAIN

Liar: or Miles on Pfeiffer

'Where she does not knowingly tell direct falsehoods, the guesses she makes about those regions that she does not visit—while stating that she does—show her to be bad at guesswork.'—Miles.

Cissy: or Locke on Locke

'What a vacillating set! I would have gone on alone had I been of the party; and therefore it is pleasing to be able to disclaim relationship with one so wanting in firmness of purpose as the author of the Home of the Eddas appears to be from this and other incidents.'—W. G. Locke.

THE 1809 REVOLUTION

(Mainly from Hooker and Mackenzie)

In the year 1808, when Great Britain was at war with Denmark, an eminent and honourable merchant of London, Mr. Samuel Phelps, learned from a young Dane of twenty-seven, Mr. Jörgen Jörgensen, that there was a large quantity of goods, chiefly tallow, for sale in Iceland. Jörgensen, though born of respectable parents, had been apprenticed on a British collier, served in the British navy, where, in his own words, he had imbibed the maxims, the principles, and the prejudices of Englishmen, and on his return to Copenhagen in 1806 had made himself unpopular by his pro-British sentiments. On the outbreak of war he had been put in command of a Danish privateer, but had been taken prisoner after an engagement off Flamborough Head with the *Sappho* and the *Clio*, landed at Yarmouth, and set free on parole.

As Iceland was wholly dependent on Denmark for necessary imports, the war was a serious matter for her, but the British, at the instigation of that exalted philanthropist Sir Joseph Banks, had given an undertaking to allow Danish merchantmen to trade unmolested with the island. These excellent intentions of His Majesty's Government were somewhat frustrated, however, by the behaviour of one of His subjects, for in 1808 a Captain Gilpin arrived in Reykjavik and made off with some 36,000 rix dollars apportioned for the relief of the poor. To return to Mr. Phelps: acting on Jörgensen's information, he commissioned a Liverpool ship, the *Clarence*, commanded by Mr. Jackson, to sail to Iceland with a cargo which, according to himself, consisted largely of necessaries, barley meal, potatoes, and salt, and according to Count Tramp, the Danish Governor of the Island, consisted largely of luxuries. Mr. Jackson undertook to molest no Danish ships under a penalty of an £8,000 fine. The *Clarence*, with Jörgensen, who omitted to mention his departure to the authorities, and an English super-cargo, Mr. Savigniac, set sail in December and landed in Reykjavik at the beginning of January 1809.

Here they discreetly showed an American flag and
American papers, but were refused permission to trade,
whereupon they hoisted the British flag, but with no
greater success. As Icelandic trade was a legal Danish
monopoly, this refusal on the part of the Danish officials
was, perhaps, not unnatural. Mr. Savigniac, however, was
determined to bring the Government to a sense of its duty
and interest, and ordered Captain Jackson to capture a
Danish brig which had just arrived. The officials capitu-
lated, and apparently gave some sort of permission, but
the Icelanders, either because they were frightened, or
because they did not want the goods—it was a bad time
of the year for business—showed no inclination to buy or
sell. So matters continued till June, when Count Tramp
returned from Copenhagen on the *Orion*. A proclamation
forbidding the Icelanders to trade with the English under
point of death which had been previously composed but
kept in a chest till his arrival was now published. Shortly
afterwards, a British man-of-war, the *Rover*, commanded
by Captain Nott, arrived, 'with the object of which in
these parts', says Count Tramp, 'I was unacquainted,
and the peaceable proceedings of which no convention
secured.' On June 16th it appears that a convention was
arrived at between Count Tramp and Captain Nott per-
mitting trade, but this agreement, though sent to the press,
was somehow never published and the existing prohibition
remained in force. The *Rover* departed, but on June 21st
Mr. Phelps arrived in person, with the *Flora* and the *Margaret and Anne*, a ship of ten guns under Captain Liston.

By June 25th Mr. Phelps had decided that 'longer
delay would be materially prejudicial to his interests, and
he must consequently be under the necessity of having
recourse to measures no more consonant to his inclinations
than to his feelings'. He seized the *Orion*, and marching with
an armed crew of twelve to the Governor's house, on Sunday

afternoon after Divine Service, arrested Count Tramp in the middle of a conversation with a Mr. Kofoed. According to his own account there were a number of Icelanders loitering about with long poles shod with iron spikes who made no attempt to resist them, in spite of the fact that 'it is sufficiently known that in times of war the crews of merchant ships consist of such men only as are unfit for the service of His Majesty.' He then asked Jörgensen to take over the government of the Island, a prospect which seems to have been highly agreeable to that young gentleman for, on the next morning, he issued a proclamation dissolving all Danish authority, confiscating all Danish property, confining all Danes to their houses, threatening all offenders against these decrees with being shot within two hours, and promising all native Icelanders 'undisturbed tranquility and a felicity hitherto unknown'. On the evening of the same day (June 26th) he issued a second proclamation by which Iceland was declared an independent republic, all debts to Denmark were repudiated, and the island was to be put in a state of defence. This last provision proved more difficult than was anticipated. A house-to-house search in Reykjavik only produced twenty to thirty old fowling pieces, most of them useless, and a few swords and pistols, so that the Icelandic army was necessarily restricted to 'eight men who dressed in green uniforms, armed with swords and pistols, and mounted on good ponies, scoured the country in various directions, intimidating the Danes, and making themselves highly useful to the new Governor, in securing the goods and property that were to be confiscated'. (The value of these varies in different accounts from 16,000 to 19,000 rix dollars.) As a further act of authority, and to show the clemency intended to be pursued, four prisoners confined in the Tught-hus were released and the place itself converted into barracks for the soldiers.

The greater part of the army was soon employed in seizing the persons of two of the civil officers, Mr. Frydensburg and Mr. Einersen, who were kept in confinement, the former for one night, the latter for eight or ten days. Hooker, who was an eye-witness of Einersen's arrest, says that 'a horse was taken for him upon which he was placed and, guarded by Jörgensen and his cavalry, was marched, or rather galloped, into the town'. Meanwhile Mr. Samuel Phelps had not been idle, but, to protect the town 'an office which he readily undertook for the security of the very considerable property he now had there', was building Fort Phelps, which he equipped with six guns that had lain buried in the sand on the shore for over 140 years.

On July 11th Jörgensen issued yet another proclamation assuming the title of his Excellency the Protector of Iceland, Commander-in-Chief by sea and land, decreeing his private seal J.J. as the official seal, and forbidding all irreverence to his person. A new flag, three split stockfish upon a dark blue ground, was hoisted for the first time on the top of a warehouse under a salute of eleven guns from the *Margaret and Anne*, and was afterwards hoisted on Sundays. Having done this, his Excellency set out on foot for the North with five of his army, and later returned with one.

All this time Count Tramp was a prisoner on board the *Margaret and Anne*, where he does not appear to have been satisfied with his treatment. 'Bent down', he says, 'under the weight of so much grief and affliction united, it now became my lot to be kept confined in a narrow and dirty cabin, and sometimes, when Captain Liston took it into his head, even shut up in a small room, or rather closet, where I was deprived of the light of the day. Constantly I was obliged to put up with the society of drunken and noisy mates, and, with them for my companions, I was reduced to exist on fare which even the men complained of as being more than commonly indifferent; in short, I

77

was deprived for the space of nine weeks, of every convenience and comfort of life to which I had been used, and subjected to all the sufferings which the oppressor had it in his power to inflict.'

These sufferings, however, were not destined to last. On August 8th occurred an event 'as unforeseen as it was unfavourable to the present state of political and commercial affairs.' The *Talbot*, commanded by the Honourable Alexander Jones, arrived in Hafnafjördur, and, after hearing both sides and deciding that 'owing to his former situation in life' Mr. Jörgensen was unwelcome to the inhabitants, arrested him for having broken his parole, restored the Danish authority, destroyed Fort Phelps, and, after a delay due to some Danes setting fire to the *Margaret and Anne*, left Iceland at the end of August with Phelps, Count Tramp, Jörgensen, and a congratulatory ode to himself composed in Icelandic and Latin by a certain Magnus Finnursson, or Finnur Magnusson, from which the following is a translated extract:

> He pretended that he served the English King: that he depended on the protection of his armies.
> He armed brothers against each other: terror seized the remainder of the people,
> Who had never before beheld the sword or blood: and unwillingly submitted to the insolent yoke.
> He, more powerful, raised fortifications: and erected his standard black as hell.
> He took a lordly title: having dared to assume possession of the supreme power.
> He pretended that our people wished for these things: and that they all demanded these tumults.

The Revolution had lasted fifty-eight days, twelve men had been employed, but not a shot fired (except in salutes) nor a sabre unsheathed.

The subsequent history of Samuel Phelps, 'who was in part to blame', is unknown, but the unfortunate Jörgensen was sent to the hulks at Chatham for a year, and was afterwards released on parole at Reading. In prison, however, it seems that he had become a confirmed gambler, and after sundry adventures was finally deported to Tasmania, where he became an explorer and a policeman. He died at Hobartstown in 1844. On February 7th, 1810, the British Government issued a decree guaranteeing the immunity of Iceland, the Faroes, and Greenland, from British attack, and encouraging British trade with these places. Count Tramp declared that 'the peculiar favour which Iceland and its concerns have met with here and the manner in which His Majesty's ministers have interested themselves in its welfare, and above all the security obtained for the future, has entirely obliterated all bitterness from my heart', but good Imperialists, like Hooker, still grumbled a little. 'England should no longer hesitate', he wrote, 'about the adoption of a step to which every native Icelander looks forward as the greatest blessing that can befall his country, and which to England herself would, I am persuaded, be productive of various signal advantages, the taking possession of Iceland and holding it among her dependencies. Iceland, thus freed from the yoke of an inefficient but presumptuous tyrant, might then, guarded by the protection of our fleets and fostered by the liberal policy of our Commercial Laws, look forward to a security that Denmark could never afford, and to a prosperity that the selfishness of the Danes has always prevented; while England would find herself repaid for her generous conduct by the extension of her fisheries, the surest source of her prosperity, and by the safety which the numerous harbours of the Island afford for her merchantmen against the storms and perils of the Arctic Ocean.'

AN ICELANDIC SUPPER IN 1809
(Hooker)

'On the cloth was nothing but a plate, a knife and fork, a wine glass, and a bottle of claret, for each guest, except that in the middle stood a large and handsome glass-castor of sugar, with a magnificent silver top. The dishes are brought in singly; our first was a large tureen of soup, which is a favourite addition to the dinners of the richer people, and is made of sago, claret, and raisins, boiled so as to become almost a mucilage. We were helped to two soup plates full of this, which we ate without knowing if anything was to come. No sooner, however, was the soup removed, than two large salmon, boiled and cut in slices, were brought on and, with them, melted butter looking like oil, mixed with vinegar and pepper; this, likewise, was very good and when we had with some difficulty cleared our plates, we hoped we had finished our dinners. Not so, for there was then introduced a tureen full of eggs of the Cree, a great tern, boiled hard, of which a dozen were put upon each of our plates; and for sauce, we had a large basin of cream, mixed with sugar, in which were four spoons, so that we all ate out of the same bowl, placed in the middle of the table. We devoured with difficulty our eggs and cream, but had no sooner dismissed our plates, than half a sheep, well roasted, came on with a mess of sorrel called by the Danes, scurvy-grass, boiled, mashed and sweetened with sugar. However, even this was not all; for a large dish of waffels as they are here called, that is to say, a sort of pancake made of wheat flour, flat, and roasted in a mould, which forms a number of squares on the top, succeeded the mutton. This was not more than half an inch thick and about the size of an octavo book. Then bread, Norway biscuit and loaves made of rye were served up: for our drink we had nothing but claret, of which we were all compelled to empty the bottle that stood by us, and this too out of tumblers rather than wine-glasses. The coffee was extremely good and we trusted it would terminate the feast; but all was not yet over; for a large bowl of rum punch was brought in and handed round in glasses pretty freely, and to every glass a toast was given. Another bowl actually came which we were with difficulty allowed to refuse to empty entirely; nor could this be done but by ordering our people to get the boat ready for our departure, when, having concluded this extraordinary feast by three cups of tea each, we took our leave and reached Reykjavik about ten o'clock, but did not for some time recover from the effects of this most involuntary intemperance.'

ERUPTION OF THE ÖRAEFAJÖKULL, 1727

(Jon. Thorlaksson, Minister of Sandfell, quoted in Mackenzie)

'In the year 1727, on the 7th August, which was the tenth Sunday after Trinity, after the commencement of divine service in the church of Sandfell, as I stood before the altar, I was sensible of a gentle concussion under my feet, which I did not mind at first; but, during the delivery of the sermon, the rocking continued to increase, so as to alarm the whole congregation; yet they remarked that the like had often happened before. One of them, a very aged man, repaired to a spring, a little below the house, where he prostrated himself on the ground, and was laughed at by the rest for his pains; but, on his return, I asked him what it was he wished to ascertain, to which he replied, "Be on your guard, Sir; the earth is on fire!" Turning, at the same moment, towards the church door, it appeared to me, and all who were present, as if the house contracted and drew itself together. I now left the church, necessarily ruminating on what the old man had said; and as I came opposite to Mount Flega, and looked up towards the summit, it appeared alternately to expand and be heaved up, and fall again to its former state. Nor was I mistaken in this, as the event shewed; for on the morning of the 8th, we not only felt frequent and violent earthquakes, but also heard dreadful reports, in no respect inferior to thunder. Everything that was standing in the houses was thrown down by these shocks; and there was reason to apprehend, that mountains as well as houses would be overturned in the catastrophe. What most augmented the terror of the people was, that nobody could divine in what place the disaster would originate, or where it would end.

'After nine o'clock, three particularly loud reports were heard, which were almost instantaneously followed by several eruptions of water that gushed out, the last of which was the greatest, and completely carried away the horses and other animals that it overtook in its course. When these exudations were over, the ice mountain itself ran down into the plain, just like melted metal poured out of a crucible; and on settling, filled it to such a height, that I could not discover more of the well-known mountain Lounagrupr than about the size of a bird. The water now rushed down the east side without intermission, and totally destroyed what little of the pasture-grounds remained. It was a most pitiable sight to behold the females crying, and my neighbours destitute both of counsel and courage: however, as I observed that the current directed its course towards my house, I removed my family up to the top of a high rock, on the side of the mountain, called Dalskardstorfa, where I caused a tent to be pitched, and all the church utensils, together with our food, clothes and other things that were most necessary, to be conveyed thither; drawing the conclusion, that should the eruption break forth at some other place, this height would escape the longest, if it were the will of God, to whom we committed ourselves, and remained there.

'Things now assumed quite a different appearance. The Jökull itself exploded, and precipitated masses of ice, many of which were hurled out to the sea; but the thickest remained on the plain, at a short distance from the foot of the mountain. The noise and reports continuing, the atmosphere was so completely filled with fire and ashes, that day could scarcely be distinguished from night, by reason of the darkness which followed, and which was barely rendered visible by the light of the fire that had broken through five or six cracks in the mountain. In this manner the parish of Oraefa was tormented for three days together; yet it is not easy to describe the disaster as it was in reality; for the surface of the ground was entirely covered with pumice-sand, and it was impossible to go out in the open air with safety, on account of the red-hot stones that fell from the atmosphere. Any who did venture out, had to cover their heads with buckets, and such other wooden utensils as could afford them some protection.

'On the 11th it cleared up a little in the neighbourhood; but the ice-mountain still continued to send forth smoke and flames. The same day I rode, in company with three others, to see how matters stood with the parsonage, as it was most exposed, but we could only proceed with the utmost danger, as there was no other way except between the ice-mountain and the Jökull which had been precipitated into the plain, where the water was so hot that the horses almost got unmanageable: and, just as we entertained the hope of getting through by this passage, I happened to look behind me, when I descried a fresh deluge of hot water directly above me, which, had it reached us, must inevitably have swept us before it. Contriving, of a sudden, to get on the ice, I called to my companions to make the utmost expedition in following me; and by this means, we reached Sandfell in safety. The whole of the farm, together with the cottages of two tenants, had been destroyed; only the dwelling houses remained, and a few spots of the tuns. The people stood crying in the church. The cows which, contrary to all expectation, both here and elsewhere, had escaped the disaster, were lowing beside a few hay-stacks that had been damaged during the eruption. At the time the exudation of the Jökull broke forth, the half of the people belonging to the parsonage were in four nearly-constructed sheep-cotes, where two women and a boy took refuge on the roof of the highest; but they had hardly reached it when, being unable to resist the force of the thick mud that was borne against it, it was carried away by the deluge of hot water and, as far as the eye could reach, the three unfortunate persons were seen clinging to the roof. One of the women was afterwards found among the substances that had proceeded from the Jökull, but burnt and, as it were, parboiled; her body was so soft that it could scarcely be touched. Everything was in the most deplorable condition. The sheep were lost; some of which were washed up dead from the sea in the third parish from Oraefa. The hay that was saved was found insufficient for the cows so that a fifth part of them had to be killed; and most of the horses which had not been swept into the ocean were afterwards found completely mangled. The eastern part of the parish of Sida was also destroyed by the pumice and sand; and the inhabitants were on that account obliged to kill many of their cattle.

'The mountain continued to burn night and day from the 8th of August, as already mentioned, till the beginning of Summer in the month of April the following year, at which time the stones were still so hot that they could not be touched; and it did not cease to emit smoke till near the end of the Summer. Some of them had been completely calcined; some were black and full of holes; and others were so loose in their contexture that one could blow through them. On the first day of Summer 1728, I went in company with a person of quality to examine the cracks in the mountain, most of which were so large that we could creep into them. I found here a quantity of saltpetre and could have collected it, but did not choose to stay long in the excessive heat. At one place a heavy calcined stone lay across a large aperture; and as it rested on a small basis, we easily dislodged it into the chasm but could not observe the least sign of its having reached the bottom. These are the more remarkable particulars that have occurred to me with respect to this mountain; and thus God hath led me through fire and water, and brought me through much trouble and adversity to my eightieth year. To Him be the honour, the praise, and the glory for ever.'

(For an account of the 1783 eruption see Nagrus Stefansson's account, quoted in Hooker, pp. 405-426.)

EXTRACT FROM SUARBAR PARISH REGISTER, 1805

Name of Farm	Name	Occupation	Age	Con-firmed	Com-muni-cant	Able to read	Conduct	General Abilities
Thyrill	Jorundur Gislasson	Constable	41	Yes	Yes	Yes	Well disposed and clean	Moderate abilities
	Margaret Thorstendottir	His wife	53	Yes	Yes	Yes	Good character	Piously disposed
	Gudrun Eireksdottir	Her daughter by a former husband	19	Yes	Yes	Yes	A hopeful girl	Well informed
	Gudrun Grimsson	Servant man	25	Yes	Yes	Yes	A faithful labourer	He has neglected his improvement and is therefore ad-monished
	Thorsdys Saensdottir	Maid-servant	42	Yes	Yes	Yes	Neat and faithful	Well informed
	Jarudur Stefansdottir	Her child	3	—	—	—	—	—
	Hristin Jonsdottir	A female or-phan	8	—	—	—	A tractable child	Has finished her cate-chism. To be con-firmed
	Waldi Sterindersson	A male orphan	6	—	—	—	Tractable and obe-dient	Is learning his cate-chism

BIBLIOGRAPHY

Arngrimur Jonsson: *Brevis Commentarius*, 1592; *Anatome Blefkeniana*, 1612; *Epistola Defensoria*, 1618; *Apotribe Calumniae*, 1622; *Chrymogea*, 1609-1630; *Specimen Islandiae*, 1643.

Blefkenius: *Islandia*, 1607.

Jonr Boty: *Treatise of the land from Iceland to Greenland* (Purchas III), 1608.

La Peyrère: *Account of Iceland* (Churchill II), 1644.

John Andersson: *Nachrichten von Island*, 1746.

*Niels Horrebow: *Nachrichten von Island*, 1750.

Tremarec: *Relation d'un voyage dans la Mer du Nord*, 1772.

*Joseph Banks and Van Troil: *Letters from Iceland*, 1772.

*Hooker: *Journal of a tour in Iceland*, 1811.

*Sir George MacKenzie: *Travels in Iceland*, 1812.

*Ebenezer Henderson: *Iceland*, 1818.

John Barrow: *A Visit to Iceland*, 1835.

Arthur Dillon: *A Winter* (1834) *in Iceland and Lapland*, 1840.

Marmier: *Lettres sur l'Islande*, 1837.

Paul Gaimard: *Voyage en Islande et au Groenland* (8 vols.), 1838-1852.

Madam Ida Pfeiffer: *A Visit to Iceland*, 1854.

Pliny Miles: *Rambles in Iceland*, 1854.

Robert Chambers: *Tracings of Iceland and the Faroe Islands*, 1856.

Charles Edmund: *Voyage dans les Mers du Nord*, 1857.

*Lord Dufferin: *Letters from High Latitudes*, 1858.

Captain Forbes: *Iceland*, 1860.

Metcalfe: *The Oxonian in Iceland*, 1861.

Symington: *Pen and Pencil Sketches*, 1862.

Baring-Gould: *Iceland, its Scenes and Sagas*, 1863.

Umbra (Clifford): *Travels*, 1865.

Shepherd: *The N.W. Peninsula of Iceland*, 1867.

Paykull: *A Summer in Iceland*, 1868.

*William Morris: *Journal*, 1871-1873.

*Viscount Bryce: *Impressions of Iceland*, 1872 (pub. 1923).

Taylor: *Egypt and Iceland*, 1874 (pub. 1902).

Richard Burton: *Ultima Thule*, 1875.

Lord Watts: *Across the Vatnajökull*, 1876.

Anthony Trollope: *How the Mastiffs went to Iceland*, 1878.

C. W. Locke: *The Home of the Eddas*, 1879.

W. G. Locke: *Askja*, 1881.

Coles: *Summer-Travel in Iceland*, 1882.

Miss Oswald: *By Fell and Fjord*, 1882.

Mrs. Alec Tweedie: *A Girl's Tour in Iceland*, 1882.

Eugène de Groote: *Island*, 1889.

Howell: *Icelandic Pictures*, 1893.

*Collingwood and Stefansson: *A Pilgrimage to the Saga-steads of Iceland*, 1899.

William Bischer: *Across Iceland*, 1902.

Annandale: *The Faroes and Iceland*, 1905.

Daniel Bruun: *Iceland. Routes over the Highlands*, 1907.

W. Russell: *Iceland. Horseback Tours in Sagaland*, 1914.

Paul Hermann: *Island. Das Land und das Volk*, 1914.

Prinz: *Das Unbekannte Island*, 1932.

Mrs. Chapman: *Across Iceland*, 1934.

*Specially recommended.

Chapter VII

Letter to R. H. S. Crossman, Esq.

———◆◆◆◆———

A glacier brilliant in the heights of summer
Feeding a putty-coloured river: a field,
A countryside collected in a field
To appreciate or try its strength;
Two flags twitter at the entrance gates.

I walk among them taking photographs;
The children stare and follow, think of questions
To prove the stranger real. Beyond the wire
The ponies graze who never will grow up to question
The justice of their permanent discipline.

Nevertheless let the camera's eye record it:
Groups in confabulation on the grass,
The shuffling couples in their heavy boots,
The young men leaping, the accordion playing.
Justice or not, it is a world.

Isn't it true however far we've wandered
Into our provinces of persecution
Where our regrets accuse, we keep returning
Back to the common faith from which we've all dissented,
Back to the hands, the feet, the faces?

89

Letter to R. H. S. Crossman, Esq.

Children are always there and take the hands
Even when they're most terrified; those in love
Cannot make up their minds to go or stay;
Artist and doctor return most often;
Only the mad will never never come back.

For doctors keep on worrying while away
In case their skill is suffering and deserted;
Lovers have lived so long with giants and elves
They want belief again in their own size;
And the artist prays ever so gently—

'Let me find pure all that can happen.
Only uniqueness is success! For instance,
Let me perceive the images of history,
All that I push away with doubt and travel,
To-day's and yesterday's, alike like bodies.'

Yes, just like that. See Gunnar killed
At Hlitharendi white across the river,
And Flosi waiting on Three Corner Ridge,
And as the dancing turns me round
The servants fighting up on Little Daimon.

But not these only, just as clearly
As them, as clearly as at the moment
The wraps of cellophane torn off
From cigarettes flit through the glass
Like glittering butterflies, I must see all.

The service yesterday among the copse of ashes,
The old men dragging hymns, the woman weeping
Leaning against her husband as he yawned;
And two days back the townee from the gasworks
Riding to Thorsmörk, highly-strung,

Loud-voiced, consumed with passion to excel
His slower-witted red-faced friend.
And see there if I can the growth, the wonder,
Not symbols of an end, not cold extremities
Of a tradition sick at heart.

For that's our vulgar error, isn't it,
When we see nothing but the law and order,
The formal interdiction from the garden,
A legend of a sword, and quite forget
The rusting apple core we're clutching still.

It's that that makes us really selfish:
When the whole fault's mechanical,
A maladjustment in the circling stars,
And goodness just an abstract principle
Which by hypothesis some men must have.

For whom we spend our idle lives in looking,
And are so lazy that we quickly find them,
Or rather, like a child that feels neglected,
Our proof of goodness is the power to punish,
We recognise them when they make us suffer.

Until indeed the Markafljöt I see
Wasting these fields, is no glacial flood
But history, hostile, Time the destroyer
Everywhere washing our will, winding through Europe
An attack, a division, shifting its fords.

Flowing through Oxford too, past dons of good will,
Stroking their truths away like a headache
Till only the unicorn and the fabulous bogey
Are real, and distinctly human only
The anarchist's loony refusing cry:—

Letter to R. H. S. Crossman, Esq.

'Harden the heart as the might lessens.
Fame shall be ours of a noble defence
In a narrow place. No choices are good.
And the word of fate can never be altered
Though it be spoken to our own destruction.'

Dear Dick,

I have just been staying in the Njàl country. I gather
the Nazis look on that sort of life as the cradle of all the
virtues. The enclosed laws and regulations seem so dotty,
I thought they might interest you.

W.

Formula of Peace-Making

1. There was feud between N. N. and M. M. but now
they are set at one and many:
> As the meter meted
> And the teller told
> And the doomsman deemed
> And the givers gave
> And the receivers received
> And carried it away
> With full fee as paid ounce
> Handselled to them that cry'd to have it.

2. Ye two shall be made men:
> At one and in agreement
> At feast and food
> At moot and meeting of the people
> At church-soken and in the king's house.
> And wheresoever men meet

Ye shall be so reconciled together as that it shall hold for
ever between you.

3. Ye two shall share knife and carven steak
   And all things between you
   As friends and not as foes.

4. If case of quarrel or feud arise between you other than is well It shall be booted or paid for with money and not by reddening the dart or arrow.

5. And he of ye twain that shall go against the settlement or atonement made
   Or break the bidden troth,
   He shall be wolf hunted, and to be hunted
   As lean as men seek wolves;
   Christian men seek churches;
   Heathen men sacrifice in temples;
   Fire burneth; earth groweth;
   Son calleth mother, and mother heareth son;
   Folk kindle fire;
   Ship saileth; snow lieth;
   The Fin skateth; the fir groweth;
   The hawk flieth the long Spring day,
   With a fair wind behind him and wings outspread;
   Heaven turneth; earth is dwelt on;
   Wind bloweth; waters fall to the sea;
   Churl soweth corn.

6. He shall be out-cast
   From Church and Christian men;
   From houses of Gods and from men,
   From every world save hell-woe or torment.

7. Now do ye two both hold one book and place the money on the book that N. N. payeth for himself and his heirs
   Born and unborn
   Begotten and unbegotten
   Named and unnamed.

8. N. N. taketh troth and truce as M. M. giveth it.
    Dear troth and strong troth
    An everlasting peace that shall hold for ever
    While the world is and men live.

9. Now are N. N. and M. M. at peace or atonement and accord wherever they meet
    On land or water
    On sea or on horseback
    To share oar and bilge scoop
    Bench and bulwark if need be
    Even set with each other
    As father with son or son with father
    In all dealings together.

Now they lay hands together, N. N. and M. M. Hold well these troths, by the will of Christ and of all those men that have now heard this form of peace:
    May he have God's grace that holdeth these troths or truce
    And he His wrath that breaketh these troths or truce
    And he have grace that holdeth them.
    Hail, ye that are set at one
    And we that are set as witnesses thereto.

Codex Regius.

Law of Wager of Battle

1. There should be a cloak of five ells in the skirt and loops at the corners. They must put down pegs with heads on one end that were called Tiosnos. He that was performing must go to the Tiosnos so that the sky could be seen between his legs, holding the lobes of his ears, with this form of words (words lost); and afterwards was performed the sacrifice that is called the Tiosno-sacrifice.

2. There must be three lines about the cloak of a foot

breadth; outside the lines there must be four posts, and they are called hazels, and the field is hazelled when this is done.

3. A man shall have three shields, and when they are gone, then he shall step on to the skin though he have left it before, and then he must defend himself with weapon henceforth.

4. He shall strike first that is challenged.

5. If one of them be wounded so that blood come on the cloak, they shall not fight any longer.

6. If a man step with one foot outside the hazels, he is said to flinch; but if he step outside with both feet, he is said to run.

7. His own man shall hold the shield for each of them that fight.

8. He shall pay ransom that is the more wounded, three marks of silver as ransom.

The Viking Law

1. No man should enter that was older than fifty and none younger than eighteen winters. All must be between these ages.

2. Never should kinship be taken into account of when they wished to enter that were not in the league.

3. No man there should run before a man of like power or like arms.

4. Every man there should avenge the other as he would his brother.

5. None then should there speak a word of fear or dread of anything, however perilous things might be.

6. All that they took in warfare should be brought to the stang or pole, little or big, that was of any value; and if a man had not done this, he must be driven out.

7. None there should kindle discussion or waken quarrel.

8. And if tidings came no man should be so rash as to tell it to anyone, but all tidings should be told to the Captain.

9. No man should bring a woman into the fort.

10. And none should be abroad three nights together.

11. And though one had been taken into fellowship that had slain father or brother of a man that was there before, or any near kinsman, and it was found out after he was received, the Captain should judge the whole case and whatever quarrel might arise between them.

12. No man should have a sword longer than an ell, so close were they to go.

13. They never took prisoners, women nor children.

14. No man should bind a wound till the same hour next day.

15. No man of them had less strength than two ordinary men.

16. It was their custom to lie ever outside the nesses.

17. It was another custom of theirs never to put awnings on their ships and never to furl the sail for the wind.

Chapter VIII

Letter to Lord Byron

PART III

My last remarks were sent you from a boat.
    I'm back on shore now in a warm bed-sitter,
And several friends have joined me since I wrote;
    So though the weather out of doors is bitter,
    I feel a great deal cheerier and fitter.
A party from a public school, a poet,
Have set a rapid pace, and make me go it.

We're starting soon on a big expedition
    Into the desert, which I'm sure is corking:
Many would like to be in my position.
    I only hope there won't be too much walking.
    Now let me see, where was I? We were talking
Of Social Questions when I had to stop;
I think it's time now for a little shop.

In setting up my brass-plate as a critic,
    I make no claim to certain diagnosis,
I'm more intuitive than analytic,
    I offer thought in homoeopathic doses
    (But someone may get better in the process).
I don't pretend to reasoning like Pritchard's
Or the logomachy of I. A. Richards.

Letter to Lord Byron

I like your muse because she's gay and witty,
    Because she's neither prostitute nor frump,
The daughter of a European city,
    And country houses long before the slump;
    I like her voice that does not make me jump:
And you I find sympatisch, a good townee,
Neither a preacher, ninny, bore, nor Brownie.

A poet, swimmer, peer, and man of action,
    —It beats Roy Campbell's record by a mile—
You offer every possible attraction.
    By looking into your poetic style,
    And love-life on the chance that both were vile,
Several have earned a decent livelihood,
Whose lives were uncreative but were good.

You've had your packet from the critics, though:
    They grant you warmth of heart, but at your head
Their moral and aesthetic brickbats throw.
    A 'vulgar genius' so George Eliot said,
    Which doesn't matter as George Eliot's dead,
But T. S. Eliot, I am sad to find,
Damns you with: 'an uninteresting mind'.

A statement which I must say I'm ashamed at;
    A poet must be judged by his intention,
And serious thought you never said you aimed at.
    I think a serious critic ought to mention
    That one verse style was really your invention,
A style whose meaning does not need a spanner,
You are the master of the airy manner.

By all means let us touch our humble caps to
    La poésie pure, the epic narrative;
But comedy shall get its round of claps, too.

According to his powers, each may give;
  Only on varied diet can we live.
The pious fable and the dirty story
Share in the total literary glory.

There's every mode of singing robe in stock,
    From Shakespeare's gorgeous fur coat, Spenser's muff,
Or Dryden's lounge suit to my cotton frock,
    And Wordsworth's Harris tweed with leathern cuff.
    Firbank, I think, wore just a just-enough;
I fancy Whitman in a reach-me-down,
But you, like Sherlock, in a dressing-gown.

I'm also glad to find I've your authority
    For finding Wordsworth a most bleak old bore,
Though I'm afraid we're in a sad minority
    For every year his followers get more,
    Their number must have doubled since the war.
They come in train-loads to the Lakes, and swarms
Of pupil-teachers study him in *Storm's*.

'I hate a pupil-teacher' Milton said,
    Who also hated bureaucratic fools;
Milton may thank his stars that he is dead,
    Although he's learnt by heart in public schools,
    Along with Wordsworth and the list of rules;
For many a don while looking down his nose
Calls Pope and Dryden classics of our prose.

And new plants flower from that old potato.
    They thrive best in a poor industrial soil,
Are hardier crossed with Rousseaus' or a Plato;
    Their cultivation is an easy toil.
    William, to change the metaphor, struck oil;
His well seems inexhaustible, a gusher
That saves old England from the fate of Russia.

The mountain-snob is a Wordsworthian fruit;
    He tears his clothes and doesn't shave his chin,
He wears a very pretty little boot,
    He chooses the least comfortable inn;
    A mountain railway is a deadly sin;
His strength, of course, is as the strength of ten men,
He calls all those who live in cities wen-men.

I'm not a spoil-sport, I would never wish
    To interfere with anybody's pleasures;
By all means climb, or hunt, or even fish,
    All human hearts have ugly little treasures;
    But think it time to take repressive measures
When someone says, adopting the 'I know' line,
The Good Life is confined above the snow-line.

Besides, I'm very fond of mountains, too;
    I like to travel through them in a car;
I like a house that's got a sweeping view;
    I like to walk, but not to walk too far.
    I also like green plains where cattle are,
And trees and rivers, and shall always quarrel
With those who think that rivers are immoral.

Not that my private quarrel gives quietus to
    The interesting question that it raises;
Impartial thought will give a proper status to
    This interest in waterfalls and daisies,
    Excessive love for the non-human faces,
That lives in hearts from Golders Green to Teddington;
It's all bound up with Einstein, Jeans, and Eddington.

It is a commonplace that's hardly worth
    A poet's while to make profound or terse,
That now the sun does not go round the earth,

That man's no centre of the universe;
    And working in an office makes it worse.
The humblest is acquiring with facility
A Universal-Complex sensibility.

For now we've learnt we mustn't be so bumptious
    We find the stars are one big family,
And send out invitations for a scrumptious
    Simple, old-fashioned, jolly romp with tea
    To any natural objects we can see.
We can't, of course, invite a Jew or Red
But birds and nebulae will do instead.

The Higher Mind's outgrowing the Barbarian,
    It's hardly thought hygienic now to kiss;
The world is surely turning vegetarian;
    And as it grows too sensitive for this.
    It won't be long before we find there is
A Society of Everybody's Aunts
For the Prevention of Cruelty to Plants.

I dread this like the dentist, rather more so:
    To me Art's subject is the human clay,
And landscape but a background to a torso;
    All Cézanne's apples I would give away
    For one small Goya or a Daumier.
I'll never grant a more than minor beauty
To pudge or pilewort, petty-chap or pooty.

Art, if it doesn't start there, at least ends,
    Whether aesthetics like the thought or not,
In an attempt to entertain our friends;
    And our first problem is to realise what
    Peculiar friends the modern artist's got;
It's possible a little dose of history
May help us in unravelling this mystery.

At the Beginning I shall *not* begin,
Not with the scratches in the ancient caves;
Heard only knows the latest bulletin
About the finds in the Egyptian graves;
I'll skip the war-dance of the Indian braves;
Since, for the purposes I have in view,
The English eighteenth century will do.

We find two arts in the Augustan age:
One quick and graceful, and by no means holy,
Relying on his lordship's patronage;
The other pious, sober, moving slowly,
Appealing mainly to the poor and lowly.
So Isaac Watts and Pope, each forced his entry
To lower middle class and landed gentry.

Two arts as different as Jews and Turks,
Each serving aspects of the Reformation,
Luther's division into faith and works:
The God of the unique imagination,
A friend of those who have to know their station;
And the Great Architect, the Engineer
Who keeps the mighty in their higher sphere.

The important point to notice, though, is this:
Each poet knew for whom he had to write,
Because their life was still the same as his.
As long as art remains a parasite,
On any class of persons it's alright;
The only thing it must be is attendant,
The only thing it mustn't, independent.

But artists, though, are human; and for man
To be a scivvy is not nice at all:
So everyone will do the best he can

To get a patch of ground which he can call
    His own. He doesn't really care how small,
So long as he can style himself the master:
Unluckily for art, it's a disaster.

To be a highbrow is the natural state:
    To have a special interest of one's own,
Rock gardens, marrows, pigeons, silver plate,
    Collecting butterflies or bits of stone;
    And then to have a circle where one's known
Of hobbyists and rivals to discuss
With expert knowledge what appeals to us.

But to the artist this is quite forbidden:
    On this point he must differ from the crowd,
And, like a secret agent, must keep hidden
    His passion for his shop. However proud,
    And rightly, of his trade, he's not allowed
To etch his face with his professional creases,
Or die from occupational diseases.

Until the great Industrial Revolution
    The artist had to earn his livelihood:
However much he hated the intrusion
    Of patron's taste or public's fickle mood,
    He had to please or go without his food;
He had to keep his technique to himself
Or find no joint upon his larder shelf.

But Savoury and Newcomen and Watt
    And all those names that I was told to get up
In history preparation and forgot,
    A new class of creative artist set up,
    On whom the pressure of demand was let up:
He sang and painted and drew dividends,
But lost responsibilities and friends.

Letter to Lord Byron

Those most affected were the very best:
    Those with originality of vision,
Those whose technique was better than the rest,
    Jumped at the chance of a secure position
    With freedom from the bad old hack tradition,
Leave to be sole judges of the artist's brandy,
Be Shelley, or Childe Harold, or the Dandy.

So started what I'll call the Poet's Party:
    (Most of the guests were painters, never mind)—
The first few hours the atmosphere was hearty,
    With fireworks, fun, and games of every kind;
    All were enjoying it, no one was blind;
Brilliant the speeches improvised, the dances,
And brilliant, too, the technical advances.

How nice at first to watch the passers-by
    Out of the upper window, and to say
'How glad I am that though I have to die
    Like all those cattle, I'm less base than they!'
    How we all roared when Baudelaire went fey.
'See this cigar', he said, 'it's Baudelaire's.
What happens to perception? Ah, who cares?'

To-day, alas, that happy crowded floor
    Looks very different: many are in tears:
Some have retired to bed and locked the door;
    And some swing madly from the chandeliers;
    Some have passed out entirely in the rears;
Some have been sick in corners; the sobering few
Are trying hard to think of something new.

I've made it seem the artist's silly fault,
    In which case why these sentimental sobs?
In fact, of course, the whole tureen was salt.

The soup was full of little bits of snobs.
The common clay and the uncommon nobs
Were far too busy making piles or starving
To look at pictures, poetry, or carving.

I've simplified the facts to be emphatic,
Playing Macaulay's favourite little trick
Of lighting that's contrasted and dramatic;
Because it's true Art feels a trifle sick,
You mustn't think the old girl's lost her kick.
And those, besides, who feel most like a sewer
Belong to Painting not to Literature.

You know the terror that for poets lurks
Beyond the ferry when to Minos brought.
Poets must utter their Collected Works,
Including Juvenilia. So I thought
That you might warn him. Yes, I think you ought,
In case, when my turn comes, he shall cry 'Atta boys,
Off with his bags, he's crazy as a hatter, boys!'

The clock is striking and it's time for lunch;
We start at four. The weather's none too bright.
Some of the party look as pleased as Punch.
We shall be travelling, as they call it, light;
We shall be sleeping in a tent to-night.
You know what Baden-Powell's taught us, don't you,
Ora pro nobis, please, this evening, won't you?

END OF PART III

Chapter IX

W. H. A. to E. M. A.—No. 1

Studentagarthurinn
Reykjavik

July 12th.

As you see, I've really got here. I didn't go to Finland after all. I felt another country would only be muddling. Finland has not the slightest connection with Iceland, and a travel book about unconnected places becomes simply a record of a journey, which is boring. I dare say it's all right if you're a neo-Elizabethan young man who has a hair-breadth escape or meets a very eccentric clergyman every five minutes, but I'm not. As it is, I've been here a month and haven't the slightest idea how to begin to write the book. Gollancz told me before I left that it couldn't be done, and he's probably right. Still the contracts are signed and my expenses paid, so I suppose it will get done. At present I am just amusing myself, with occasional twinges of uneasiness, like a small boy who knows he's got an exam to-morrow, for which he has done no work whatsoever.

I spent a very miserable first week here, for all the people I had introductions to were away. Reykjavik is the worst possible sort of provincial town as far as amusing oneself is concerned, and there was nothing to do but soak in the only hotel with a license; at ruinous expense. There is a would-be English band there with a leader looking like a stage gigolo, and real revolving coloured lights in the ballroom after ten. But as it is broad daylight all night the effect is rather depressing. Gradually I began to meet people, so that my head is reeling with gossip that I know is libellous, and information that I suspect of being unreliable.

I hear, for instance, that such and such a politician is either the first gentleman in Iceland or is suffering from persecution mania since he was laughed at by some children at the ski-club, that such and such a professor pawned his marriage lines the day before the wedding, that such and such a girl is a 'levis avis', that the German consul has smuggled in arms in preparation for a Putsch, that the Icelanders cannot discipline their children, that England is the true home of spiritualism, and that the only good drinks are whisky and vermouth.

My own personal impressions don't go far yet. There is no architecture here and the public statues are mostly romanticised Galahad-Vikings. The King of Denmark has paid a visit and I watched him come out of the prime minister's house accompanied by distinguished citizens. I know top-hats and frock coats don't make people look their best, but on their appearance alone I wouldn't have trusted one of them with the spoons. He went to see the Great Geysir, which refused to oblige, and the current rumour gives as the reason that out of national pride they fed it with local soap instead of the Sunlight brand to which it is accustomed.

The other excitement has been a Swedish students' week. They gave a concert, to which I went. They sang well enough, but the songs were dull—none of the polyphonic kind which I like. The concert opened oddly. One of the students on the platform put on white gloves and a yachting cap, and took hold of an enormous flag. As they began to sing what I presume was the Swedish National Anthem as everyone stood up, he brought the flag smartly to the present. I'm sure it was much too heavy for him. The song over he took off his gloves and his hat, stood the flag in the corner, and joined the rest of the choir. It all looked very pompous and silly, more what one would expect from the Nazis than from a sensible Scandinavian democracy.

After the second song a bouquet was brought in for the conductor; I hoped that this was just to encourage him, and that they would bring in a new and better one after each song till the platform was like a greenhouse, but I was disappointed.

I've been to Thingvellir, the stock beauty spot, which is certainly very pretty, but the hotel is full of drunks every evening. A very beautiful one called Toppy asked me to ring her up when I got back.

Last week I went down into the country and had a nice time riding, but I can't tell you about that now as I must pack ready to set off to-morrow for the North. How I wish you were here to help me, as you know how I hate it. This hotel is all right, but not up to your standard of course. It's a hostel for university students in the winter. The furniture is of that cosmopolitan modern sort you find in the waiting-rooms of all European air-ports. Snags—the food which is often cold and the bath which won't work. The proprietor is a nice man who tells me that he is a practical idealist and that his children have perfect characters. I'll try and go on with this to-morrow.

Hraunsnef. July 15th

A game of rummy prevented me writing last night, but now there is an hour or so before the bus is due and I am tired of helping with the hay, which I have been doing since breakfast.

One of the nice things about Iceland is its small size, so that everything is personal. A steam roller is called a

Briett after a well-known feminist with deformed feet. I had a proof of this on Monday morning when I was going to catch the bus. A man I had never seen before stopped me in the street and said 'There are some letters for you', took me along and unlocked the post office specially for my benefit. How he knew I was leaving town I don't know. Among them were the proofs of my poems, so I can occupy odd moments by trying to put in logical punctuation, which is something I don't understand. I can only think of them as breathing indications. I hope you will approve of the dedication. They are due out in October, which is a pity, as they will be eclipsed by the posthumous volume of Housman which is due for then.

I wonder very much what there'll be in it. There was a nice quatrain going about the Oxford Senior Common Rooms before I left England which he is said to have woken up reciting to himself:

> When the bells jussle in the tower
>   The hollow night amid
> Then on my tongue the taste is sour
>   Of all I ever did.

I've been trying to find out something about modern Icelandic poetry. As far as I can make out there has been no break since the Romantic Revival, which got here via Denmark and Germany, i.e., no 'modernist' poetry to puzzle the old ladies. Technically it is of a very high standard, rhyme, assonance, and alliteration are all expected. As a Latin example of an Icelandic verse structure I was given the following, which you can recite to any dirty-minded don you meet.

> Theodorus tardavit
> Tempore non surrexit
> Violare voluit
> Virginem non potuit.

They seem to have preserved a passion for ingenuity helped by their damnably inflected language, since the days of the Scald's, whose verse would have broken St. John Ervine right up. Even now they write palindrome verses which can be read forwards or backwards, like this:

Falla tímans voldug verk   Daga alla stendur sterk
    varla falleg baga.   Studla ríman snjalla
Snjalla ríman studla sterk   Saga falleg varla verk
    Stendur alla daga.   voldug tímans falla.

Sentiment: Art is long and life is short or life is short and art is long. Or verses like this in which the second half is made up of the beheaded words of the first:

Snuddar margur trassin   Many a lazy idler lounges
    traudur   And finds the day long;
    Treinist slangur daginn   The wicked one rubs his red
Nudda argur rassin raudur   bottom
    reinist langur aginn.   And finds discipline irksome

Another peculiar thing about Icelandic verse is the persistence of a genuine poetic language. In the following, for instance, which is the equivalent of a double entendre limerick like 'The young people who frequent picture palaces', the first word for girl is as 'poetic' as demoiselle.

Yngissveinar fara a fjöll
    Finnar sprund i leynum
Stilkar elska atlaf böll
    astfangnar af sveinum.

The proper version is:

Young men go to embrace girls in secret
Girls love to go to the ball
In love with the young men.

But what has struck me most is that any average educated person one meets can turn out competent verse. When I

was down in the South, I had an Icelandic student as
companion; I gave him one of the ruthless rhymes:

> When baby's cries grew hard to bear
> I popped him in the Frigidaire.
> I never would have done so if
> I'd known that he'd be frozen stiff.
> My wife said 'George, I'm so unhappé,
> Our darling's now completely frappé.'

In twenty minutes he came back with this, which as far as
I can make out is pretty literal.

> Grenjar kenja krakkinnmin
> Eg kasta honum i snjóskaflin
> Eg thetta medal fljótast finn
> Thá frys á honum kjafturinn
> En sidan kveinar kerlingin
> Ad króknad hafi ánginn sinn.

He also translated a serious poem of mine which I'm sorry
to say I've lost but it sounded grand. I in return have been
trying to teach them the Clerihew, and there are now, I
hope, many little boys going about saying

> Jonathan Swift
> Never went up in a lift,
> Neither did Robinson Crusoe
> Do so.

I recited to my present companion, Ragnar, who is a mine
of information about songs and proverbs, a touching little
cri du cœur made by a friend:

> I think that I would rather like
> To be the saddle of a bike

only to find that the Icelandic equivalent in terms of
horses already exists.

We are staying at a little farm under a cliff, called

Hraensnef or Lava Nose, in Nordara, which is one of the
great salmon fishing rivers, bought up of course and let
to Harley Street surgeons and popular novelists. We
started at eight o'clock yesterday morning. The buses are
comfortable but the roads are not, and we hadn't gone ten
miles before some of the passengers started to be sick. The
driver tells me that the Icelanders always are. We
stumbled along round a spectacular fjord called Hvalf-
jordur over a track that would have been rough going on
foot, passing historical sites like the island from which a
pirate's wife escaped her enemies by swimming to shore with
her two children on her back, and the farm where a seven-
teenth-century clergyman called Peterssen wrote some famous passion hymns and died of leprosy, until we stopped for
coffee at a little inn full of bad oil paintings and surrounded
by bedraggled hens. In the last fifteen years or so there has
grown up quite a school of Icelandic painters, and their
work is to be found in all inns, schools, and public buildings.
I've seen some heads by a man called Kjarval which I
liked, one or two other landscapes by various people, and
a farmer's own portrait of his mother; but Cézanne has
done them no good. I suppose I should also say that we
saw a pair of eagles. They looked far too heavy to fly.

We got to Hredavatn—a little lake about a mile and a
half away, where we intended to stop—about half-past
two, but the inn was full so we came on here, which is
much better situated. Behind is a great escarpment of rock
and to the left a cone-shaped mountain called Beula which
looks fine from this distance, but I am glad I haven't got
to climb it. To the right are some small craters which look
as if they had been made the day before yesterday, as they
are as destitute of vegetation as the slag heap of an iron
foundry, and are surrounded by a tiny lava field which
stops suddenly in the middle of the morass, like jam spilt
out of a bowl.

The sitting-rooms of Icelandic farms are all rather alike. Like English cottages they are crammed with furniture and knick-knacks; there are pictures on the walls, and a bowl of picture postcards and snapshots of the family on the table, and there is always a harmonium. Unfortunately the music is nearly always the same, a book of psalm tunes and a book of songs something like Gaudeamus, all rather pom po pom pom. Here, however, I've found 'Moonlight in the Sahara' but, alas, the vox humana won't work. The family consist of the farmer and his wife, an unmarried and rather spoilt daughter, a very independent son of eleven in a fetching red shirt, a little boy of four, the child of a relation, and a boy who is helping with the harvest and looks seventeen but is only fourteen. They are very hospitable and friendly.

Yesterday morning we spent riding, and to my great joy I got a really frisky horse who bucked and galloped as hard as one could wish. I got a scare once when we were going up the steep side of a valley and he started to slip.

In the afternoon we rode to Hredavatn and took a boat on the lake. It turned out a wonderful evening and we sat on an island and threw stones and waved at a girl in a bungalow on the shore. It took us about an hour to catch Ragnar's horse again, which tried to kick or bite when you came anywhere near it, but got home at last and spent the evening playing rummy, which I like because you can talk while you play. Svava, the daughter, had all the luck, and I discover that I am a very bad loser.

Ragnar is bothering me to come and pack, as the bus should be here any minute.

Sandakrökur

We caught the Icelandic Train Bleu all right. Two coaches crammed to capacity. How embarrassing it is to get into an already crowded bus when the passengers have got to know each other. We felt like the Germans invading Belgium. But the atmosphere soon thawed; I got my travelling rug well over my knees, found that my cigarettes had come out of their packet into my pocket, and settled down as an accepted citizen of a temporary regime.

In the front where the bunches of canvas flowers were, sat the élite, including an immense woman in a tiger skin coat. At the back where the bumps were at a maximum sat ourselves. In front of me a man with a convict's face looking very green, and next to me a man looking like Thomas Hardy. Presently the singing began. Two of the commonest tunes in Iceland are ones we know to Integer Vitae, and God save the King. Ragnar turned out to have a nice baritone, to know more songs, and to have more self-confidence than the others, so he led the singing while I fumbled for bass parts and occasionally got them. There was one long song about a person called Melakoff who I gather drank brandy and revived when the doctor began to dissect him.

I've got some gramophone records of more primitive local music, including an amazing one of a farmer and two children who yell as if they were at a football match. These are much more interesting; some of the music reminds me of the sort of intoning you get at a Jewish service, and with a curious prolonging of the final note.

The hills are all covered in mist. Road menders peered out of wayside tents, bridge sides suddenly shaved the bus. Loud cries of excitement told that someone had hit his head very hard on the roof at a bump. Thomas Hardy offered me some snuff and the bus roared when I sneezed. Now we were passing through a district of terminal moraines which looked too like the illustrations in a geography text book to be real. Here the last public execution took place in the early nineteenth century. Sweets were passed round. Sick streamed past the windows.

At four o'clock we reached Blonduos, a one-horse sort of place, where we were to have lunch. Everyone clattered off to their respective lavatories and then down to the dining-room, where I was lucky to arrive early enough to get a real chair instead of a bench. The first course was rice and raisins and ginger. I could have wept, I was so hungry. And the rest was scarcely better, enormous hunks of meat that might have been carved with a chopper smeared with half-cold gravy. No one can accuse the Icelander of being dainty. I watched a large man opposite leisurely stuffing down large pieces of tepid fat like the hero of a Sunday-school story.

On again, grinding over a watershed, up test gradients. The view from the top is said to be one of the best in the island, but it wasn't to-day. We came down to Vidamyri, where stands the oldest church in Iceland. Unfortunately we didn't stop, and I only caught a glimpse of it, squat and turf covered, like a shaggy old sheep with a bell round its neck. Shortly afterwards we reached the crossroads where we were to change horses. There was a hurricane blowing and the temperature outside wasn't far off freezing. As I paid the driver a ten krónur note blew away and I had to chase it for a hundred yards. The bus from Akureyri had also arrived, and Ragnar was talking to one of his old school-masters. I got into the primitive local bus and tried to get warm. Luckily it was only forty minutes or so to Sanda-krökur, and we got there at eight. It might have been built by Seventh Day Adventists who expected to go to heaven in a few months, so why bother anyway. I have no wish to see it again. The inn is dirty, and smells like a chicken run. The proprietor has a wen on his face and charges 6 kr. a day. In my room are two embroidered samplers—*Blessed be the Lord* and *Blest are the pure in heart*—and an inferior print of Iceland's first fishing ship, dated 1876.

After supper I went to call on the local doctor, to whom I had an introduction. A very nice man with a face like a lizard, and a very keen diet crank. He has a hospital here and is very interested in cancer, the recent increase of which in Iceland he attributes to imported foods and too much sugar. He says the annual consumption of sugar per head is 80 lb. Came back to an early bed. The fishing ship creaked all night.

Decided to get out of this place as soon as possible, but it was not as easy as it sounded. A milk cart was due to leave for Holar at 2. It left at 5.30. There were three of us on a seat made for two, Ragnar, myself, and a gigantic red-faced consumptive boy. We stopped every five minutes to dump empty cans by the road side. Both my feet were sound asleep by the time we reached Holar: a church, a farm, and a large white agricultural school in the depths of a spectacular valley. The young Danish headmaster of the school welcomed us, and we sat and listened to the wireless while supper was prepared. Someone apparently has tried to assassinate King Edward VIII. Nobody looked very interested. Supper was poor, and we played rummy till bedtime with the consumptive and another boy with a bandaged finger. I scored 270 in one hand and was very pleased with myself.

Holar was the seat of a bishopric, and I spent the next morning in the church, which is as ugly as most protestant places of worship. The only relic of the past is the carved altar piece. I strummed on the harmonium, and balanced books and hassocks on the altar candlesticks, and stood on the altar in my socks and struck matches trying to photograph the carving. Mysterious violent figures rise out of the background slashing at prisoners without looking at them. Impassive horses survey another world than theirs. One of the thieves has his head thrown right back and on his forehead dances a bear holding a child. Serried figures, the Queen of Heaven with a tower, St. Peter with no back to his head etc., rise like a Greek Chorus, right and left of the main panel. After lunch we got a couple of rather obstinate horses and started up the valley intending to visit the glacier at its head. It was a brilliant sunny day and we didn't get half way, but lay on the grass dozing and teasing a couple of bell spiders with a straw.

Great excitement here because Goering's brother and a party are expected this evening. Rosenberg is coming too. The Nazis have a theory that Iceland is the cradle of the Germanic culture. Well, if they want a community like that of the sagas they are welcome to it. I love the sagas, but what a rotten society they describe, a society with only the gangster virtues.

I saw Goering for a moment at breakfast next morning, and we exchanged politenesses. He didn't look in the least like his brother, but rather academic.

The milk cart back to Sandakrökur was worse than the first because we had to collect full cans. It took us four hours to go forty-two kilometres, and I had run out of cigarettes so just sulked into my waistcoat.

We didn't get away again till eight in the evening, but got through the afternoon somehow. We looked over the cheese works, a friendly place, not too efficient nor too clean, thank God. Two workmen were ragging about spinning each other round on a turntable. An old woman came in with a basket on her arm and begged for some cream. The doctor took me over his hospital and showed me the apple of his eye, his new X-ray apparatus. Most of the patients were very old women. A younger one who had had a cancerous breast removed the week before sat in a rocking chair and said she felt better. A surgeon's fees are not princely. 100 kr. for the removal of a breast, 50 kr. for an appendicotany, 18 kr. for amputating a finger. General practitioners get a small allowance from the state, but as they have to pay for their own dispensing, it must be hard to make ends meet. Chloroform is little used, and in the country districts the midwife has to act as anaesthetist.

The commonest complaints are T.B., cancer, and gastric ulcer.

We went back to the doctor for dinner. He may be a food crank but he has a very good table. He made us try two Icelandic specialities, old shark and whale pickled in sour milk, eccentric but not absolutely inedible. I smoked, but a little guiltily, as on his shelves were a number of books on the evils of tobacco. Time passed quickly enough as I got down some of his surgical books to read.

We got to our little farm Ulfstadur at last, about 11 p.m., to find a hot meal waiting for us, and went straight to bed.

Owing to some breakdown in the telephone system, the bus next morning had not been warned and was too full to take us, so we had to wait till the evening. Went riding in the morning, and pottered about in the afternoon. There was a lovely view from the lavatory. The bus came along about five and we didn't get to Akureyri till half-past eleven. Some of the passengers had bottles and were tight. Once we stopped for coffee and once we all had to get out, to cross a bridge the piles of which had sunk, making it unsafe. Ragnar was at school in Akureyri and was besieged by acquaintances the moment we arrived. It would be nice to be greeted like that at Victoria or Paddington. All the hotels were full and I was in rather a quandary, but a fair-haired artist friend of Ragnar's, one of a family of sixteen, had a butcher brother-in-law who was away, and we went off to his house, one of the new concrete ones, and made ourselves a meal of eggs and tea at one o'clock in the morning, feeling excited like sham burglars.

Monday

Went down to the Hotel Gullfoss for breakfast and looked round Akureyri, which is a much nicer town than Reykjavik. Unfortunately there is a fish factory to the north and to-day the wind is blowing from the north. There is a boat in the harbour going to Greenland on a geological expedition, loading up horses and fodder. With its single narrow funnel, its tall masts, and its crow's nest, it looks like an illustration out of a nine-teenth-century adventure story. I went up to the school to see its collection of Icelandic paintings. They may not be very wonderful, but at least they are of interest to the Icelanders.

The artists are trying to amuse their friends, and their friends are not only artists. The pictures are not canned art from a Paris store which the locals must take because there is no other.

In the afternoon I had my hair cut and called on a lawyer, who gave me a whisky and cigar. We talked about capital punishment, beating, and boarding-schools. In the evening I went with a party of students to the only dance hall. The Blue Boy Band were deafening and never stopped playing for a second. Sweat poured off our faces. 'A pity about Berg's death,' I roared. But the band assured us all that the music goes round and round. A few tables off were the Greenland expedition, some of them half-caste Danish Eskimos. The eskimo features seem dominant. I stood it for about an hour and then went to bed.

Tuesday

I worked all this morning and finished a poem on Iceland at last, or rather it's about the voyage out and better, I hope, than William Morris's effort.

The only other one I've done is about why people read detective stories. Here it is.

Detective Story

For who is ever quite without his landscape,
The straggling village street, the house in trees,
All near the church, or else the gloomy town house,
The one with the Corinthian pillars, or
The tiny workmanlike flat: in any case
A home, the centre where the three or four things
That happen to a man do happen? Yes,
Who cannot draw the map of his life, shade in
The little station where he meets his loves
And says good-bye continually, and mark the spot
Where the body of his happiness was first discovered?

An unknown tramp? A rich man? An enigma always
And with a buried past—but when the truth,
The truth about our happiness comes out
How much it owed to blackmail and philandering.

The rest's traditional. All goes to plan:
The feud between the local common sense
And that exasperating brilliant intuition
That's always on the spot by chance before us;
All goes to plan, both lying and confession,
Down to the thrilling final chase, the kill.

Yet on the last page just a lingering doubt
That verdict, was it just? The judge's nerves,
That clue, that protestation from the gallows,
And our own smile . . . why yes . . .

But time is always killed. Someone must pay for
Our loss of happiness, our happiness itself.

After lunch I went to bathe in what must be one of the
most northerly open-air swimming baths in the world. It

is fed from a hot spring and as the day was sunny and windless most attractive. The standard of swimming here is high and there was one first-class diver. I cannot conceive of anything else I would rather be able to do well. It's such a marvellous way of showing off.

Have just heard for the first time of the civil war in Spain. Borrowed two volumes of caricatures, which are really my favourite kind of picture, and spent a very happy evening with Goya and Daumier and Max Beerbohm, only slightly marred by the consciousness of a sore throat, which means one of my foul colds to-morrow.

I'll get this off in the post to-morrow morning, as I shan't be able to get another one posted for several days, I expect, but I'll write something every day and get it posted when I can.

W.

Chapter X

Eclogue from Iceland

Scene: The Arnarvatn Heath. Craven, Ryan, and the ghost of Grettir. Voice from Europe.

R.   This is the place, Craven, the end of our way;
    Hobble the horses, we have had a long day.

C.   The lake is said to be full of trout;
    A pity the mist shuts the glacier out.

R.   There used to be swans but the frost last year
    Has brought their numbers down round here.

C.   I like this place. My personal choice
    Is always to avoid the public voice.

R.   You are quite right, Craven. For people like us
    This is an enviable terminus.

C.   To stay here a week like a placid brute
    To explore the country, to fish and shoot.

R.   That would be life, not having to shave,
    Clocking in as a wage-slave.

C.   That would be life, Ryan, that would be life,
    Without kowtowing to boss or wife.

R.   And beside this cold and silicate stream
    To sleep in sheepskin, never dream,

C.   Never dream of the empty church,

R.   Nor of waiting in a familiar porch
    With the broken bellpull, but the name
    Above the door is not the same.

C.   And never wake to the maid's knock

R.   Nor to the sour alarum clock,

C.   Miss the faces fed at eight
       And the daily paper on your plate,

R.   And miss the pile of letters from
       Forgotten Bill and ailing Tom.

C.   Stop a moment. I think I hear
       Someone walking over there.

R.   Hell, Craven. Who could it be?
       Except the echo of you and me.

C.   There is someone there just out of sight—
       Will probably camp here to-night.

R.   It is a damn bore anyhow.
       Look. There he is coming now.
       The mist makes him look so big
       And he is limping in one leg.

G.   Good evening, strangers. So you too
       Are on the run? I welcome you.
       I am Grettir Asmundson,
       Dead many years. My day is done.
       But you whose day is sputtering yet—
       I forget. . . . What did I say?
       We forget when we are dead
       The blue and red, the grey and gay.
       Your day spits with a damp wick,
       Will fizzle out if you're not quick.
       Men have been chilled to death who kissed
       Wives of mist, forgetting their own
       Kind who live out of the wind.
       My memory goes, goes— Tell me
       Are there men now whose compass leads
       Them always down forbidden roads?
       Greedy young men who take their pick
       Of what they want but have no luck;
       Who leap the toothed and dour crevasse

Of death on a sardonic phrase?
You with crowsfeet round your eyes,
How are things where you come from?

C.   Things are bad. There is no room
To move at ease, to stretch or breed—

G.   And you with the burglar's underlip,
In your land do things stand well?

R.   In my land nothing stands at all
But some fly high and some lie low.

G.   Too many people. My memory will go,
Lose itself in the hordes of modern people.
Memory is words; we remember what others
Say and record of ourselves—stones with the runes.
Too many people—sandstorm over the words.
Is your land also an island?
There is only hope for people who live upon islands
Where the Lowest Common labels will not stick
And the unpolluted hills will hold your echo.

R.   I come from an island, Ireland, a nation
Built upon violence and morose vendettas.
My diehard countrymen, like drayhorses,
Drag their ruin behind them.
Shooting straight in the cause of crooked thinking
Their greed is sugared with pretence of public
      spirit.
From all which I am an exile.

C.   Yes, we are exiles,
Gad the world for comfort.
This Easter I was in Spain, before the Civil War,
Gobbling the tripper's treats, the local colour,
Storks over Avila, the coffee-coloured waters of
      Ronda,
The comedy of the bootblacks in the cafés,
The legless beggars in the corridors of the trains,
Dominoes on marble tables, the architecture

     Moorish mudejar churriguerresque,
     The bullfight—the banderillas like Christmas
          candles,
     And the scrawled hammer and sickle:
     It was all copy—impenetrable surface.
     I did not look for the sneer beneath the surface.
     Why should I trouble, an addict to oblivion,
     Running away from the gods of my own hearth
     With no intention of finding gods elsewhere?

R.   And so we came to Iceland—
C.   Our latest joyride.
G.   And what have you found in Iceland?
C.   What have we found? More copy, more surface,
     Vignettes as they call them, dead flowers in an
          album—
     The harmoniums in the farms, the fine-bread and
          pancakes
     The pot of ivy trained across the window,
     Children in gumboots, girls in black berets.
R.   And dead craters and angled crags.
G.   The crags which saw me jockey doom for twenty
     Years from one cold hide-out to another;
     The last of the saga heroes
     Who had not the wisdom of Njàl or the beauty of
          Gunnar,
     I was the doomed tough, disaster kept me witty;
     Being born the surly jack, the ne'er-do-well, the
          loiterer,
     Hard blows exalted me.
     When the man of will and muscle achieves the
          curule chair
     He turns to a bully; better is his lot as outlaw,
     A wad of dried fish in his belt, a snatch of bil-
          berries
     And riding the sullen landscape far from friends

Through the jungle of lava, dales of frozen fancy,
Fording the gletcher, ducking the hard hail,
And across the easy pastures, never stopping
To rest among the celandines and bogcotton.
Under a curse I would see eyes in the night,
Always had to move on; craving company
In the end I lived on an island with two others.
To fetch fire I swam the crinkled fjord,
The crags were alive with ravens whose low croak
Told my ears what filtered in my veins—
The sense of doom. I wore it gracefully,
The fatal clarity that would not budge
But without false pride in martyrdom. For I,
Joker and dressy, held no mystic's pose,
Not wishing to die preferred the daily goods
The horse-fight, women's thighs, a joint of meat.

C.   But this dyspeptic age of ingrown cynics
Wakes in the morning with a coated tongue
And whets itself laboriously to labour
And wears a blasé face in the face of death.
Who risk their lives neither to fill their bellies
Nor to avenge an affront nor grab a prize,
But out of bravado or to divert ennui
Driving fast cars and climbing foreign mountains.
Outside the delicatessen shop the hero
With his ribbons and his empty pinned-up sleeve
Cadges for money while with turned-up collars
His comrades blow through brass the Londonderry
     Air
And silken legs and swinging buttocks advertise
The sale of little cardboard flags on pins.

G.   Us too they sold
The women and the men with many sheep.
Graft and aggression, legal prevarication
Drove out the best of us,

Secured long life to only the sly and the dumb
To those who would not say what they really
    thought
But got their ends through pretended indifference
And through the sweat and blood of thralls and
    hacks,
Cheating the poor men of their share of drift
The whale on Kaldbak in the starving winter.

R.   And so to-day at Grimsby men whose lives
Are warped in Arctic trawlers load and unload
The shining tons of fish to keep the lords
Of the market happy with cigars and cars.

C.   What is that music in the air—
Organ-music coming from far?

R.   Honeyed music—it sounds to me
Like the Wurlitzer in the Gaiety.

G.   I do not hear anything at all.

C.   Imagine the purple light on the stage,

R.   The melting moment of a stinted age,

C.   The pause before the film again
Bursts in a shower of golden rain.

G.   I do not hear anything at all.

C.   We shall be back there soon, to stand in queues
For entertainment and to work at desks,
To browse round counters of dead books, to pore
On picture catalogues and Soho menus,
To preen ourselves on the reinterpretation
Of the words of obsolete interpreters,
Collate, delete, their faded lives like texts,
Admire Flaubert, Cézanne—the tortured artists—
And leaning forward to knock out our pipes
Into the fire protest that art is good
And gives a meaning and a slant to life.

G.   The dark is falling. Soon the air
Will stare with eyes, the stubborn ghost

	Who cursed me when I threw him. Must
	The ban go on forever? I,
	A ghost myself, have no claim now to die.
R.	Now I hear the music again—
	Strauss and roses—hear it plain.
	The sweet confetti of music falls
	From the high Corinthian capitals.
C.	Her head upon his shoulder lies. . . .
	Blend to the marrow as the music dies.
G.	Brought up to the rough-house we took offence
	quickly
	Were sticklers for pride, paid for it as outlaws—
C.	Like Cavalcanti, whose hot blood lost him Florence
R.	Or the Wild Geese of Ireland in Mid-Europe.
	Let us thank God for valour in abstraction
	For those who go their own way, will not kiss
	The arse of law and order nor compound
	For physical comfort at the price of pride:
	Soldiers of fortune, renegade artists, rebels and
	sharpers
	Whose speech not cramped to Yea and Nay ex-
	plodes
	In crimson oaths like peonies, who brag
	Because they prefer to taunt the mask of God,
	Bid him unmask and die in the living lightning.
	What is that voice maundering, meandering?
VOICE.	Blues . . . blues . . . high heels and manicured hands
	Always self-conscious of the vanity bag
	And puritan painted lips that abnegate desire
	And say 'we do not care' . . . 'we do not care'—
	I don't care always in the air
	Give my hips a shake always on the make
	Always on the mend coming around the bend
	Always on the dance with an eye to the main
	Chance, always taking the floor again—

C.   There was Tchekov,
        His haemorrhages drove him out of Moscow,
        The life he loved, not born to it, who thought
        That when the windows blurred with smoke and
            talk
        So that no one could see out, then conversely
        The giants of frost and satans of the peasant
        Could not look in, impose the evil eye.

R.   There was MacKenna
        Spent twenty years translating Greek philosophy,
        Ill and tormented, unwilling to break contract,
        A brilliant talker who left
        The salon for the solo flight of Mind.

G.   There was Onund Treefoot
        Came late and lame to Iceland, made his way
        Even though the land was bad and the neighbours
            jealous.

C.   There was that dancer
        Who danced the war, then falling into coma
        Went with hunched shoulders through the ivory
            gate.

R.   There was Connolly,
        Vilified now by the gangs of Catholic Action.

G.   There was Egil,
        Hero and miser, who when dying blind
        Would have thrown his money among the crowd
            to hear
        The whole world scuffle for his hoarded gold.

C.   And there were many
        Whose common sense or sense of humour or mere
        Desire for self assertion won them through

R.   But not to happiness. Though at intervals
        They paused in sunlight for a moment's fusion
        With friends or nature till the cynical wind
        Blew the trees pale—

VOICE.   Blues, blues, sit back, relax,
              Let your self-pity swell with the music and clutch
              Your tiny lavendered fetishes. Who cares
              If floods depopulate China? I don't care
              Always in the air sitting among the stars
              Among the electric signs among the imported
                  wines
              Always on the spree climbing the forbidden tree
              Tossing the peel of the apple over my shoulder
              To see it form the initials of a new intrigue,
G.   Runes and runes which no one could decode,
R.   Wrong numbers on the 'phone—she never
                  answered.
C.   And from the romantic grill (Spanish baroque)
              Only the eyes looked out which I see now.
G.   You see them now?
C.   But seen before as well.
G.   And many times to come, be sure of that.
R.   I know them too
              These eyes which hang in the northern mist, the
                  brute
              Stare of stupidity and hate, the most
              Primitive and false of oracles.
C.   The eyes
              That glide like snakes behind a thousand masks—
              All human faces fit them, here or here:
              Dictator, bullying schoolboy, or common lout,
              Acquisitive women, financiers, invalids,
              Are capable all of that compelling stare,
              Stare which betrays the cosmic purposelessness
              The nightmare noise of the scythe upon the hone,
              Time sharpening his blade among high rocks alone.
R.   The face that fate hangs as a figurehead
              Above the truncheon or the nickelled death.
G.   I won the fall. Though cursed for it, I won.

C.   Which is why we honour you who working from
              The common premisses did not end with many
              In the blind alley where the trek began.

G.   Though the open road is hard with frost and dark.

VOICE. Hot towels for the men, mud packs for the women
              Will smooth the puckered minutes of your lives.
              I offer you each a private window, a view
              (The leper window reveals a church of lepers).

R.   Do you believe him?

C.   I don't know.
              Do you believe him?

G.   No.
              You cannot argue with the eyes or voice;
              Argument will frustrate you till you die
              But go your own way, give the voice the lie,
              Outstare the inhuman eyes. That is the way.
              Go back to where you came from and do not keep
              Crossing the road to escape them, do not avoid the
                    ambush,
              Take sly detours, but ride the pass direct.

C.   But the points of axes shine from the scrub, the
                    odds
              Are dead against us. There are the lures of women
              Who, half alive, invite to a fuller life
              And never loving would be loved by others.

R.   Who fortify themselves in pasteboard castles
              And plant their beds with the cast-out toys of
                    children,
              Dead pines with tinsel fruits, nursery beliefs,
              And South Sea Island trinkets. Watch their years
              The permutations of lapels and gussets,
              Of stuffs—georgette or velvet or corduroy—
              Of hats and eye-veils, of shoes, lizard or suède,
              Of bracelets, milk or coral, of zip bags,
              Of compacts, lipstick, eyeshade, and coiffures

All tributary to the wished ensemble,
The carriage of body that belies the soul.

C.   And there are the men who appear to be men of
        sense,

Good company and dependable in a crisis,
Who yet are ready to plug you as you drink
Like dogs who bite from fear; for fear of germs
Putting on stamps by licking the second finger,
For fear of opinion overtipping in bars,
For fear of thought studying stupefaction.
It is the world which these have made where dead
Greek words sprout out in tin on sallow walls—
Clinic or polytechnic—a world of slums
Where any day now may see the Gadarene swine
Rush down the gullets of the London tubes
When the enemy, x or y, let loose their gas.

G.   My friends, hounded like me, I tell you still
Go back to where you belong. I could have fled
To the Hebrides or Orkney, been rich and famous,
Preferred to assert my rights in my own country,
Mine which were hers for every country stands
By the sanctity of the individual will.

R.   Yes, he is right.

C.   But we have not his strength,

R.   Could only abase ourselves before the wall
Of shouting flesh,

C.   Could only offer our humble
Deaths to the unknown god, unknown but wor-
        shipped,
Whose voice calls in the sirens of destroyers.

G.   Minute your gesture but it must be made—
Your hazard, your act of defiance and hymn of
        hate,
Hatred of hatred, assertion of human values,
Which is now your only duty.

C.   Is it our only duty?

G.   Yes, my friends.
What did you say? The night falls now and I
Must beat the dales to chase my remembered acts.
Yes, my friends, it is your only duty.
And, it may be added, it is your only chance.

L. M.

Chapter XI

W. H. A. to E. M. A.—No. 2

Akureyri.

Wednesday

I was right. My throat is much worse, like a lime kiln. I don't know whether this stage is the most unpleasant or the next, when I shall cry for two days. Most disfiguring and embarrassing and I've only got one handkerchief. I suppose my It is really repenting its sins, which it apparently has to do about every six months, but I wish it wouldn't. I caught the nine o'clock bus to Myvatn, full of Nazis who talked incessantly about Die Schönheit des Islands, and the Aryan qualities of the stock 'Die Kinder sind so reizend: schöne blonde Haare und blaue Augen. Ein echt Germanischer Typus.' I expect this isn't grammatical, but that's what it sounded like. I'm glad to say that as they made this last remark we passed a pair of kids on the road who were as black as night. In the corner was a Danish ornithologist with a pursed little mouth, like a bank clerk who does a little local preaching in his spare time, who answered a Danish girl next to him in explosive monosyllables as if he were unused to talking and couldn't moderate his voice. Two more hikers got in, Austrians this time, and then a German ornithologist with a guide who looked a cross between Freud and Bernard Shaw. For the

first time I have struck a dud bus. It developed a choke in
the petrol feed and got slower and slower. We got to the
Godafoss and I had some coffee while the Germans went
to admire. One waterfall is extraordinarily like another.
We didn't get to Myvatn till three o'clock and I was
hungry and seedy and cross. The lake is surrounded by
little craters like candle snuffers and most attractive. Hay
was being made everywhere and the haymakers were using
aluminium rakes, which I have never seen before. I had to
make arrangements for an old German and his beautiful
daughter who knew no English or Icelandic, who wanted to
go to Dettifoss but didn't know if they dare. Papa was
afraid it was too much for daughter, and daughter that it
was too much for Papa, especially the horses. As he can't
have weighed a pound under 16 stone, it is the horses who
should worry. Afterwards I lay in the sun watching the
hay being made and taking photographs. If I can get them
developed in time, and any of them come out, I'll send
you some. It's a pity I am so impatient and careless, as any
ordinary person could learn all the technique of photography in a week. It is *the* democratic art, i.e. technical
skill is practically eliminated—the more fool-proof cameras
become with focusing and exposure gadgets the better—
and artistic quality depends only on choice of subject.
There is no place for the professional still photographer,
and his work is always awful. The only decent photographs are scientific ones and amateur snapshots, only you
want a lot of the latter to make an effect. A single still is
never very interesting by itself. We started back about
five, more crowded than ever, and the petrol stoppage
much worse. We stopped to fill up and I was very annoyed
because I was the wrong side of the bus to take the farmer's girl working the pump, which would have made a
beautiful Eisenstein sort of shot. The bus got weaker and
weaker and I thought we were going to run backwards

down a hill. A lot of passengers got off at a school, thank
goodness, and we tottered home, back-firing all the way,
with a magnificent sunset over the mountains, and got in
about ten. I went to eat and then ran into some drunk
Norwegian sailors. An Icelandic acquaintance of theirs
passed and greeted one by slapping him on the bottom,
which started a furious argument conducted entirely in
English, something like this.

— Why did you do that?

— Why shouldn't I?

— Don't you know it's an insult to slap a man on his
arse?

— No, it isn't.

— Yes, it is.

— No it isn't. It's an Icelandic custom.

— Oh no, it isn't.

— How do you know?

— How do I know. Everybody knows.

— No, they don't.

— I tell you it's an insult to slap a chap's arse.

— How can you tell me when you don't know about
Iceland?

— If you don't know that, you're goddam uneducated.

— How should I know that when I know it isn't.

   (Two officers stroll up and stand by. The crowd
   begins to disperse.)

— Well, be more careful, next time, Mister, see.

— Same to you.

Thursday

Left at 8 a.m. for the east. The first part of the way
was the same as yesterday. A couple were drawing nets
out of a lake like a scene in the New Testament. At Godafoss one of the real professional English travellers got in,
something I shall never be, handsome, sunburnt, reserved,

speaking fluent Icelandic. Got to Husavik for lunch. A beautiful bay and much sun. On the pier herring gutting was in full swing; great beefy women standing up to their ankles in blood and slime, giving free demonstrations of manual dexterity. My cold has rolled over into the next stage and I am beginning to weep. After Husavik the road branched off into the desert and there were still large patches of snow on the stones, the remains of a particularly severe winter, looking as if a small boy had got loose with the whitewash. I amused myself by identifying the pictures. There was Australia, and there was Italy, and that one surely was meant to be Arthur Balfour. We crossed an estuary plain and stopped to look at Asbyrgi, a vaulted horseshoe-shaped ravine about two miles long, said to have been made by Odin's horse Sleipnir when he slipped. Ragnar pointed out a house to me where lived a painter who has a platonic passion for the Dettifoss and spends his days painting it.

After Asbyrgi the condition of the road defies description. Two ruts full of stones. Thank God there are only four of us in the bus. We can just manage about 5 m.p.h., first through a sort of scrub like the horrible country where O.T.C. field days are always held, then through absolute desert, sand and rocks, like the uninteresting and useless débris of an orgy. My cold keeps boiling over like a geysir. Hours pass. The lights are lovely. Now we are worming like a beetle through sandhills, sandhills of every shape, the pincushion, the carrot, the breaking wave. We sit swaying like sacks. Nobody speaks. About ten we get to Grimstadur, the farm where we are stopping the night. A bag of lime has burst in the luggage compartment and percolated into my pack. I watched the farmer's family crowding round him as he stood against a wall in the dusk and read the newspaper we had brought him. We had supper and tumbled into bed.

Friday

Lovely weather still, but my cold is still streaming so that I can't look anybody in the face. The country is a wide flat plain spotted with steep little hills and ridges. Herdubreid, looking with its glacier on the top like a large iced cake, stands up ahead of us, and far in the distance you can catch a glimpse of the Vatnajökull, the big icefield in the south. The road is better now and we get along quite quickly. We stop for a moment at the next large farm, Morduradalur, which is renowned for its home-made ale and a drunken clergyman. The country clergy here are all farmers as well, which brings them in touch with their parishioners, but perhaps rather secularises them. But I fancy that religion has never been very enthusiastic in Iceland. The church organisation certainly must have been the one thing which civilised the social structure of the settlers, but I can't picture Iceland producing St. Francis or St. Theresa.

I found a nice little story in the Faroe saga.

Thora asked him what teaching his foster-father had given him on Holy Writ. Sigmund said he had learnt his paternoster and creed. Thora said—I would like to hear it! On which he sang his paternoster, as she thought, pretty well. But Sigmund's creed ran thus—

> Given to us are angels good,
> Without them go I ne'er a foot;
> Where'er I am, where'er I fare
> Five angels follow everywhere.
> Paltering prayer, if so I be,
> To Christ they bear them presently:
> Psalms, too, seven can I sing—
> Have mercy on me, God my King.

'At this moment Thrand comes into the room and asks what they are talking about. Thora answers and says her son has been rehearsing the Christian knowledge he had taught him. But the creed seems to be wrong! "Ah!" said Thrand, "Christ, you know, had twelve disciples or more, and each of them had his own credo. Now I have my credo, and you have the credo you have been taught; there are many credos, and they may be right without being exactly the same." And with that the conversation ended.'

We crossed the watershed and came down to Skjoldolfs-stadur for a not very good lunch. Sweet soup, which I will not eat, and hot smoked mutton, which I can only just get down. Then on to Egilsstadur for tea where I say good-bye to Ragnar and get off. Egilsstadur is one of the largest farms in Iceland and the first place where I have got really good food. It has a private cemetery on a little hill, surrounded by birch trees, but private cemeteries aren't allowed any more. I went and looked at a fine bull, which looked absurdly like a film director I know called Arthur Elton, and then found the lavatory, which opens into a lower barn, giving such an updraught that the paper flies up instead of down and I had to chase it like a moth.

In the bus to-day I had a bright idea about this travel book. I brought a Byron with me to Iceland, and I suddenly thought I might write him a chatty letter in light verse about anything I could think of, Europe, literature, myself. He's the right person I think, because he was a townee, a European, and disliked Wordsworth and that kind of approach to nature, and I find that very sympathetic. This letter in itself will have very little to do with Iceland, but will be rather a description of an effect of travelling in distant places which is to make one reflect on one's past and one's culture from the outside. But it will form a central thread on which I shall hang other letters to different people more directly about Iceland.

Who the people will be I haven't the slightest idea yet, but I must choose them, so that each letter deals with its subject in a different and significant way. The trouble about travel books as a rule, even the most exciting ones, is that the actual events are all extremely like each other—meals—sleeping accommodation—fleas—dangers, etc, and the repetition becomes boring. The usual alternative, which is essays on life prompted by something seen, the kind of thing Lawrence and Aldous Huxley do, I am neither clever enough nor sensitive enough to manage.

I hope my idea will work, for at the moment I am rather pleased with it. I attribute it entirely to my cold. It is a curious fact how often pain or slight illness stimulates the imagination. The best poem I have written this year was written immediately after having a wisdom tooth out.

Saturday

The weather has broken at last and it is cold and pouring wet. I consoled myself with the harmonium. There is more music here than usual, and my rendering of the Air on the G string was very moving, but I came to grief on a gavotte or a trumpet suite. One of the more curious jobs in this world must be inventing attractive names for harmonium stops, particularly for the tremolo. In this country I have seen it called: Vox humana—Aeolean harp—Vox seraphicum—Vox celeste and Cor angelicus.

Went for a short walk in the afternoon to the bridge over the half-lake, half-river which fills this valley. I was thinking about a picture of the seven ages of man I saw in some book or other. A girl playing a flute to a young man, two infants wrestling in a meadow, and an old man staggering to a grave, you know the kind of thing. After tea the thoughts developed into a poem.

O who can ever praise enough
The world of his belief?
Harum-scarum childhood plays
In the meadows near his home;
In his woods love knows no wrong;
Travellers ride their placid ways;
In the cool shade of the tomb
Age's trusting footfalls ring.
O who can paint the vivid tree
And grass of fantasy?

But to create it and to guard
Shall be his whole reward.
He shall watch and he shall weep,
All his father's love deny,
To his mother's womb be lost.
Eight nights with a wanton sleep,
But upon the ninth shall be
Bride and victim to a ghost,
And in the pit of terror thrown
Shall bear the wrath alone.

A rich tradesman and family from Reykjavik have arrived. Unpleasant. Smug with money and no manners. The children keep whispering.

Sunday

Still wet, but my cold is much better. Worked at the Byron letter in the morning and after lunch, thank goodness, the rich people went away. I asked for a horse and did I get one! The farmer gave me his own, which is the prize race horse of East Iceland. He came with me and we had a marvellous ride. I didn't start too well, as when I mounted in a confined courtyard with a lot of other horses near, I clucked reassuringly at him, which sent him prancing round, scattering people and horses in all directions. I was rather frightened, but got on all right after that. The moment we got on the road, we set off at full gallop, and on the last stretch home I gave him his head and it was more exciting than a really fast car. The farmer said, 'You've ridden a lot in England, I expect.' I thought of my first experience at Laugavatn a month ago, and how I shocked an English girl by yelling for help, I thought of the day at Thingvellir when I fell right over the horse's neck when getting on in full view of a party of picnickers. This was my triumph. I was a real he-man after all. Still, Ronald Firbank was a good horseman. And what about those Scythians.

Spent the evening playing rummy with the farmer's children, a girl of fourteen with an extravagant squint, and two boys of twelve and eight, all charming. I hope to go up to the valley to Hallormastadur to-morrow.

Monday

Arrived here safely this afternoon. This place is a school in the winter to teach girls weaving and cooking. The headmistress is the image of Queen Victoria and rather formidable, but I think she will thaw.

Staying here is a Scotch girl, an English lecturer at one of our provincial universities, and a great Icelandophil. She thinks them like the Greeks. Terribly enthusiastic, rushing at life like a terrier. I wonder if she really enjoys herself as much as she protests. I can imagine her in a siege saying at dinner, 'What? Fried rats? Goody. How awfully exciting.' But she is intelligent and extremely good-hearted.

Tuesday

I found an excellent collection of German songs and spent the morning playing them. Really, they choose funny things to cheer themselves up with. How about this for a soldier's song?

> Die bange Nacht ist nun herum
> Wir reiten still, wir reiten stumm
> Wir reiten ins Verderben.

I found a nice nursery song from Saxony:

> Hermann, fla larman
> Fla pipen, fla trummen
> Der Kaiser will kummen
> Mit Hammer und Stangen
> Will Hermann uphangen.

It's a great pleasure to think that all the best nursery poetry shocks the Neo-Hygienic-child-lover. There's an Icelandic lullaby for instance:

> Sofúr thu svind thitt
> Svartur i áugum
> Far i fulan pytt
> Fullan af dráugum

which means, I think:

> Sleep, you black-eyed pig.
> Fall into a deep pit full of ghosts.

I also found a magnificent Dance of Death, which I expect you know, but I had never seen before, and which seems very topical. I like the grammar lesson in the last line:

> Der Tod reit' oft als General
> Beim Trommel und Kanonschall.
> Er gibt Parol, du musst ihm nach
> Ins Bivouac bis zum letzen Tag.

> Als klapperdürrer Musikant
> Zieht er durch Deutschland und welsche Land
> Und wenn er geigt, tanzt alles geschwind,
> Der Mann, das Weib, der Bursch, das Kind.

The book belongs to a German lady who married an Icelander, solely, as far as I can see, in order to have a child, as she left him immediately after, and now won't go back to Germany. She had a magazine from the Race Bureau of the N.S.D.P. which was very funny. Boy-scout young Aryans striding along with arms swinging past fairy-story negroes and Jews.

In the afternoon we rode over the lake to Brekka, where the local doctor lives, and had tea. A romantic evening sky over the lake but unfortunately no romance.

Wednesday

Still fine but beginning to cloud over, and we shall have rain before nightfall. I have just blistered both my hands by helping the busman to pump up a tyre with a dud pump, which is annoying, as I shan't be able to ride for several days. The only other people staying here are a couple of Dutch schoolmarms, intelligent, well dressed, and attractive, a great contrast to the English variety. They have seen the Pfeffermühle, I'm glad to say, and were very impressed. By the way, I've finished that sketch with the goose for Thérèse. I haven't got a copy as it's appearing in the next volume of *New Writing*, but I'll send you a proof copy as soon as it comes. I hope it will suit her.

Reykjavik, Sunday, August 9th

It's a very long time since I added anything to this letter, but I have been absorbed in the Byron letter. I've finished a draft of the first canto and bits of the second and third. My trouble is that the excitement of doing a kind of thing I've never tried to do before keeps making me think it's better and funnier than it is, which is the reverse of what I usually find.

I drove over last Sunday from Egilsstadur in the farmer's car to Seydisfjordur, where there was a sport-fest. The farmer and his wife have been very good to me. He is a power in the new farmers' party, which represents the richer ones, who want to lower wages and increase the price of meat. For the first time in my life I have become a wireless fan. I suppose it is due to being alone in a foreign country. I listen to everything from England, even the cricket matches and the Stock Exchange quotations. I wish I knew how things were really going in Spain. Do write and tell me if you know anything authentic.

There was still a lot of snow on the hills round Seydisfjordur, really deep drifts in places and snow bridges over the streams. The sport-fest was a primitive affair. Some part singing by middle-aged men in blue suits with brass buttons which was barely audible, male and female high jumping, and a swimming race in a shallow and very dirty-looking pond. I decided to stay in the town till Wednesday, when the *Nova* was due to arrive—by which I've come round the north back to Reykjavik—and put up at the home for decayed old ladies. The landlady had travelled a little and was snobbishly pleased to see me; but snobbish or not, she was kindness itself, and kept making dishes that she thought I should like—pies and French salads. Among her collection of post-cards was a remarkable diagram of the Icelandic mountains, which I stole, as I want to reproduce it in the book. Half the inmates were in bed dying, but those that were up were odd enough. An old postman and his wife crippled with arthritis, a lady who has fits of violent mania and paper tearing, but unfortunately not while I was there, a dipsomaniac, and an old man with the face of a saint who has a month to live (cancer). He has been a servant all his life to a farmer's widow who never paid his wages, made him sleep on the floor, and whenever he had any new clothes said 'Those are too good for you. What do you want with fine things like that?' and gave them away.

The only comedian in Iceland arrived and gave a performance in a tent, patter songs and the Ruth Draper kind of imitations. As far as I could judge he was rather good. The audience howled with pleasure. While I was wandering about in the early hours of the morning waiting for the *Nova*, I ran into him. He was rather tight. He gave me a copy of his book of songs and told me many times how wonderful he was.

The boat was almost empty. There was a young American who had just taken his law finals and was having his last fling in Europe, one of those Americans who read everything, from poetry to anthropology and economics, with apparently no preferences; and a Norwegian fish merchant of twenty-four (looking nineteen) who runs his own business, and tells me you can't trust the Icelandic business man a yard.

I find voyages so boring that I can hardly remember a thing. The discipline was not aggressive and we could wander on to the bridge whenever we liked. The captain was charming and told us all about his children and their illnesses. He has only once got off the boat to go on shore in Iceland and that was to have a bath. He has a stock phrase:'I must'nt spoil my girlish figure.' There was a selfish little English gentleman of independent means at Akureyri who said, apropos of Spain, 'Why can't these foreigners behave themselves. It's sickening. You can't travel anywhere nowadays without running into trouble,' and told me the French had no sense of discipline.

There were delicious pickled pigs' trotters to eat at dinner. And that's about all I remember except the whaling station at Talknafjördur. O no it isn't. I had a nightmare after reading a silly book on spiritualism. I woke up sweating and wrote it down there and then in the middle of the night, but now I can hardly decipher what I wrote. I was in hospital for an appendix. There was somebody

there with green eyes and a terrifying affection for me. He
cut off the arm of an old lady who was going to do me an
injury. I explained to the doctors about him but they were
inattentive, though presently I realized that they were
very concerned about his bad influence over me. I decide
to escape from the hospital, and do so after looking in
a cupboard for something, I don't know what. I get to a
station, squeeze between the carriages of a train, down a
corkscrew staircase and out under the legs of some boys
and girls. Now my companion has turned up with his
three brothers (it may have been two). One, a smooth-
faced, fine fingernailed blonde, is more reassuring. They
tell me that they never leave anyone they like and that
they often choose the timid. The name of the frightening
one is Giga (in Icelandic *Gigur* is a crater) which I associate
with the name Marigold and have a vision of pursuit like
a book illustration and I think related to the long red-
legged scissor man in *Shockheaded Peter*. The scene changes
to a derelict factory by moonlight. The brothers are there,
and my father. There is a great banging going on which
they tell me is caused by the ghost of an old aunt who lives
in a tin in the factory. Sure enough the tin, which resembles
my mess tin, comes bouncing along, and stops at our feet,
falling open. It is full of hard-boiled eggs. The brothers are
very selfish and seize them, and only my father gives me
half his.

I wish I could describe things well, for a whale is the
most beautiful animal I have ever seen. It combines the
fascination of something alive, enormous, and gentle, with
the functional beauties of modern machinery. A seventy-
ton one was lying on the slip-way like a large and very
dignified duchess being got ready for the ball by beetles.
To see it torn to pieces with steam winches and cranes is
enough to make one a vegetarian for life.

In the lounge the wireless was playing 'I want to be bad'

and 'Eat an apple every day'. Downstairs the steward's canary chirped incessantly. The sun was out; in the bay, surrounded by buoys and gulls, were the semi-submerged bodies of five dead whales: and down the slip-way ran a constant stream of blood, staining the water a deep red for a distance of fifty yards. Someone whistled a tune. A bell suddenly clanged and everyone stuck their spades in the carcase and went off for lunch. The body remained alone in the sun, the flesh still steaming a little. It gave one an extraordinary vision of the cold controlled ferocity of the human species.

I got back here this afternoon about tea-time, and have been trying to read through my enormous pile of correspondence. I hope to get back to England about the middle of September. Louis has arrived but is still out seeing the Great Geysir. Now I have to make arrangements for this Bryanston party who arrive at the end of the week. Michael is coming with them and I hope he will stay on with Louis and me. It will be nice having some company for a change. To-morrow I have to give an interview to the press. I'm enclosing some oddments which may interest you; the fairy story which I came across again here used to be my favourite when I was small and my father used to read it to me. If it hadn't been for this story I don't suppose I should be here now.

W.

Proverbs

A step-child will never get so well into the bosom but the feet will hang out.

Ale is another man.

Better drink from a beaker than from bent palms.

Better turn back while the car can run.

Between friends a narrow creek; between relations a wide fjord.

Bridals for young, barrows for old.

Dull edge and point should only carve soft meat.

Every man likes the smell of his own farts.

Fear not raven at rest, nor ragged old man.

Folk are found even over the fells.

Gifts should be handed, not hurled.

He that falls will seldom fatten.

If mending will do, why cut off.

It's hard to bring many heads under one hat.

It is merely a transition, said the fox, when they flayed him alive.

Land is ruled by lip, sea by hand.

Love your neighbour but let his gate stand still.

Many a person thinks me like himself.

Many meet who made no tryst.

Many secrets are hidden in a fog.

Many tell of St. Olaf who never saw him.

Men fight by day, devils by night.

No one becomes a bishop without a beating.

One must cultivate the oak under which one has to live.

Only those who have it can splash the skyr about.

Pissing in his shoe keeps no man warm for long.

Shameless is the robber that first seeks a settlement.

Tend the sapling; cut down the old oak.

The best muck is the mould that falls from the master's shoes.

The child brought up at home who has been nowhere, knows nothing.

The haddock never wanders wide, but it has the same spot by its side.

The meanest guest has keenest eye.

The oak gets what another tree loses.

The water is deep indeed for the old mare when the young foal has to swim.

The wolf has made friends before now of fighting swine.

They can't all have the bishop for their uncle.

Too bland is a blemish; too bluff greater.

Gellivör

Near the end of the Roman Catholic times a certain married couple lived at a farm named Hvoll, situated on a firth in the east part of the country. The farmer was well to do, and wealthy in sheep and cattle. It was commonly reported that a female troll lived on the south side of the firth, who was supposed to be mild and not given to mischief.

One Christmas Eve, after dark, the farmer went out and never returned again, and all search for him was in vain. After the man's disappearance one of the servants took the management of the farm, but was lost in the same manner, after dark on the Christmas Eve following. After this the widow of the farmer determined to remove all her goods from the house and live elsewhere for the winter, leaving only the sheep and herds under the charge of shepherds, and returning to pass the summer there. As soon as the winter approached she made preparations for leaving Hvoll, until the next spring, and set the herdsmen to take care of the sheep and cattle, and feed them during the cold season.

For home use she always kept four cows, one of which had just had a calf.

Two days before her intended departure, a woman came to her in her dreams, who was dressed in an old-fashioned dress of poor appearance. The stranger addressed her with these words: 'Your cow has just calved, and I have no hope of getting nourishment for my children, unless you will

150

every day, when you deal out the rations, put a share for me in a jug in the dairy. I know that your intention is to move to another farm in two days, as you dare not live here over Christmas, for you know not what has become of your husband and of the servant, on the last two Christmas Eves. But I must tell you that a female troll lives in the opposite mountains, herself of mild temper, but who, two years ago, had a child of such curious appetite and disposition that she was forced to provide fresh human flesh for it each Christmas. If, however, you will do willingly for me what I have asked you to do, I will give you good advice as to how you may get rid of the troll from this neighbourhood.'

With these words the woman vanished. When the widow awoke she remembered her dream, and getting up, went to the dairy, where she filled a wooden jug with new milk and placed it on the appointed spot. No sooner had she done so than it disappeared. The next evening the jug stood again in the same place, and so matters went on till Christmas.

On Christmas Eve she dreamt again that the woman came to her with a friendly salutation, and said, 'Surely you are not inquisitive, for you have not yet asked to whom you give milk every day. I will tell you. I am an elf-woman, and live in the little hill near your house. You have treated me well all through the winter, but henceforth I will ask you no more for milk, as my cow had yesterday a calf. And now you must accept the little gift which you will find on the shelf where you have been accustomed to place the jug for me; and I intend, also, to deliver you from the danger which awaits you to-morrow night. At midnight you will awake and feel yourself irresistibly urged to go out, as if something attracted you; do not struggle against it, but get up and leave the house. Outside the door you will find a giantess standing, who will seize you and carry you in her arms across your grass-field, stride over the river, and make off with you in the direction of the mountains in which she lives. When she has carried you a little way from the river, you must cry, "What did I hear then?" and she will immediately ask you, "What did you hear?" You must answer, "I heard someone cry, 'Mamma Gellivör, Mamma Gellivör!'" which she will think very extraordinary, for she knows that no mortal ever yet heard her name. She will say, "Oh, I suppose it is that naughty child of mine," and will put you down and run to the mountains. But in the meantime, while she is engaged with you, I will be in the mountain and will thump and pinch her child without mercy. Directly she has left you, turn your back upon the mountain and run as fast as you possibly can towards the nearest farm along the river banks. When the troll comes back and overtakes you, she will say, "Why did you not stand still, you wretch?" and will take you again in her arms and stride away with you. As soon as you have gone a little way you must cry again, "What did I hear then?" She will ask as at first, "What did you hear?" Then you shall reply again, "I thought I heard someone calling 'Mamma Gellivör, Mamma Gellivör!'" on which she will fling you down as before, and run towards the mountain. And now you must make all speed to reach the nearest church before she can catch you again, for if she succeed in doing so she will treat you horribly in her fury at finding that I have pinched and thumped her child to death. If, however, you fail in getting to the church in time, I will help you.'

When, after this dream, the widow awoke, the day had dawned, so she got up and went to the shelf upon which the jug was wont to stand. Here she found a large bundle, which contained a handsome dress and girdle and cap, all beautifully embroidered.

About midnight on Christmas Day, when all the rest of the farm people at Hvoll were asleep, the widow felt an irresistible desire to go out, as the elf woman had warned her, and she did so. Directly she had passed the threshold, she felt herself seized and lifted high in the air by the arms of the gigantic troll, who stalked off with her over the river and towards the mountain. Everything turned out exactly as the elf had foretold, until the giantess flung down her burden for the second time, and the widow made speed to reach the church. On the way, it seemed to her as if someone took hold of her arms and helped her along. Suddenly she heard the sound of a tremendous land-slip on the troll's mountain, and turning round saw in the clear moonlight the giantess striding furiously towards her over the morasses. At this sight she would have fainted with fear had she not felt herself lifted from the ground and hurried through the air into the church, the door of which closed immediately behind her. It happened that the priests were about to celebrate early mass, and all the people were assembled. Directly after she came into the church the bells began to ring, and the congregation heard the sound of some heavy fall outside. Looking from one of the windows they saw the troll hurry away from the noise of the bells, and, in her flight, stumble over the wall of the churchyard, part of which fell. Then the troll said to it, 'Never stand again,' and hurrying away took up her abode in another mountain beyond the confines of the parish of Hvoll.

Chapter XII

Hetty to Nancy

Gullfoss.

August 17th (Monday I think, but you can't be sure in these parts.)

Dearest Nancy,

How are you and I hope you are liking the Dolomites —it was the Dolomites, wasn't it—and what about your new girl-friend? I thought she sounded sweet but that may be just by contrast. With the last I mean; I warned you about her all along and what can one expect of someone who reads botany? You keep to the Arts, darling, though in Cambridge I suppose even the Arts are just a teeny bit marked with the beast—all this psychology and politics. Now don't *you* go and get political, because that would be the last straw. The hammer and sickle are all right where they belong but they don't suit lady dons. Oh dear, I am writing under such difficulties—that was Maisie gave me a kick then. Not intentional; it's the size of them you know. Maisie Reynolds, in case you think I mean Maisie Goldstein. Well, I am writing in a frightful tent made by Maisie's sister-in-law when she was convalescent. She must have been very ill, I think. We are going round a thing called the Langjökull; if you want to pronounce it you must move your mouth both ways at once, draw your tongue through your uvula, and pray to St. David of Wales.

Lang means long and jökull means glacier; depressing
don't you think? Why we are doing this I can't imagine
and if we had to do it, *why, oh why* like this? Here am I
with Maisie in a tent and on our left side is another tent
and on our right side is another tent. And what do you
think are in those tents? SCHOOLGIRLS! Would you
believe it? Robin will think I am returning to my vomit.
He already holds it a great blot on my character, my having been a school-marm. Well, Maisie said it would be
much cheaper to have these girls along. They were all
fixed up with guides, you see. So I in a moment of weak-
ness agreed to it. Four girls—Ruth, Anne, Mary, and
Stella—and a marm called Margery Greenhalge. They are
really quite possible, poor dears, but I mean, *I mean,
darling*, does one come to Iceland for this? It's all very well
for Maisie; it's copy for her, she's writing a new book
about a schoolmistress who hanged herself, but when this
pack of girls gets in The Great Open Spaces goodness
knows what is going to happen. Sprained ankles is the
least I should think (they've none of them ever ridden
horses; nor have I for that matter). Talking of the G.O.
Spaces Maisie says they are a closed book. I have been
wondering if this would be considered an epigram because
I couldn't see that it was very funny and Maisie is supposed to be witty, but then it is different in London, where
people have always been drinking sherry before you say
anything to them. It is a pity you don't know Maisie
though or you would see the joke of all this. Which brings
me back to this tent. M. says it is my own fault for not
bringing a tent of my own. Hers is a minute conical affair
stuck up on a collapsible, not to say collapsing, umbrella-
handle which comes (very much so) to pieces, three of
them, and one of them we lost of course, it being already
getting dark (Heavens what grammar!) so when you get
it up in the end it is not more than five foot across but that

gives you quite a wrong impression of amplitude because, as I said, it is a cone and it narrows so quickly that even when Maisie and I are on our hands and knees we can only talk to each other round the back of each other's heads— do you see what I mean—and goodness knows how we are going to sleep in it. M. says it would be all right if she were by herself as she always sleeps in the foetal position but sleeping in the foetal position means curling herself round the axle-tree (that *is* the word, isn't it) and I am just not going to have Maisie encroaching on my half of ground-sheet, it's not as if she were petite after all, still I have to try and be nice about it as Maisie has been rather vexed with me. You see, she never made it clear that she expected me to turn up for this expedition equipped with one of everything—one fork, one knife, one spoon, one cup, one plate—so naturally I came with none of everything because I thought they were provided by the company. But it seems not. I must try and become more like Miss Greenhalge, who has organised her little flock beautifully, they all have cups and knives and their tents look just like tents, which is more than Maisie's does. I don't mind the shape or the colour so much though Maisie's scores a blob on both but what really galls me is that the girls' tents have doors which lace up all snug and comfy whereas this thing has a large triangular hole in it open to the breeze and nothing to cover it. Maisie has brought a very flashy pneumatic mattress with her, yellow on one side and blue on the other, she looked like something out of Brueghel blowing it up but it does look definitely comfortable; I have only got a second-hand sleeping-bag, Miss Greenhalge calls it a flea-bag (Miss Greenhalge is one of those people who when in Rome insist on talking Roman) *my* bag was left behind by an explorer—doesn't that make one feel the real thing—and it had a corkscrew in it which seemed odd but Maisie says nothing need surprise you from

an explorer and she is going to write a book about explorers
some time called The Pole of Solitude. I am writing this
by a candle. Maisie is holding it. The night outside is
damp. Doubly damp in fact, (*a*) because there is a Scotch
mist, (*b*) because in our efforts to do the right thing from
the start we have pitched camp on the edge of a ravine
and in the spray of a large waterfall. This waterfall is called
Gullfoss. I am told that foss is also the Icelandic for bicycle
because when they introduced the bicycle the natives
could think of nothing except a waterfall sufficiently
velocitous to compare it with. Anyhow it is a very fine
waterfall as waterfalls go but, as Maisie says, they don't
go far. One of the girls, Mary, has a ciné-camera and took
some photos of it in the twilight. Maisie is getting tired of
holding the candle but I must just get down the events of
the day for you. This morning we met our girls in Reykjavik and took them buying oilskins. Miss G. wanted also
to do the sights but we dissuaded her. There is only one
real sight in Reykjavik and that is a museum of sculpture
by a man called Einar Jonsson. The worst sculpture I have
ever seen in my life, and that is saying a lot. First of all all
the pieces are in plaster and you know how filthy plaster
gets, secondly they are all, or nearly all, *enormous*, thirdly
they are symbolic. And the symbolism, darling, is the sort
they used to have in the Academy before someone put
their foot down or was it the effect of the war? You know
—Time pulling off the boots of Eternity with one hand
while keeping the wolf from the door with the other. The
only one which didn't seem to be symbolic was Queen
Victoria on an elephant; a welcome piece of naturalism as
Maisie remarked. So we didn't take the girls to this cor-
rupting spectacle but they had a look round the shops of
the great city Reykjavik and most of the things are imported from England, raspberry - coloured baths and
mauve lavabos, but there was one window of home-made

Icelandic pottery which for some odd reason (or perhaps influenced by Einar Jonsson's Victoria) consists mainly of mantelpiece figures of elephants. This reminds me that we asked someone why Beatrix Potter shouldn't be done in Icelandic and they said, 'But the children wouldn't know any of the animals.' Which is true—frogs, squirrels, rabbits—you just don't find those things here. Well, all the time we were looking at these novelties of civilisation (comparative novelties here though I even saw some Elizabeth Arden preparations and also heard some children singing The Music Goes Round and Around in Icelandic which also no doubt is culture pace Hitler who wants to reclaim this island and will no doubt substitute the Eddas for the Lutheran prayerbook) Maisie, who is an indefatigable interviewer, was interviewing a Social Democrat whom I saw at parting, a lost soul M. says—was the first socialist here and is ending in sorry compromise. All I noticed was the colour scheme of his hands—dark brown to deep orange, strong black hair on them, and very light pink fingernails. So we shook off the dust of that city and took our bus for Gullfoss. What giggling, my dear! The bus was a combination bus and lorry. In the bus-part sat ourselves—a *merry* little company—and in the lorry-part sat our packs and food. The food is much but odd— 10 kilograms of smoked mutton (Hāngikýll in Icelandic, you'd never guess how that's pronounced), Miss Greenhalge by the way doesn't use the word Icelandic, she calls it the local lingo, 10 long loaves of brown bread, brick-hard, the sort of thing you find in Egyptian tombs, a vast dried mat of Hardfiskur (dried fish), two enormous slabs of cheese (4 kilos each I think), 10 large tins of mutton. It seems a lot but we have to feed the guides as well—two guides, nice men but they have no English. Well, as we bussed it, we turned aside to look at a small geysir called Grylla which spouts of itself every two hours through a small round hole in a flat stone. Of course we didn't know when the two hours were due so we had to wait. There were sundry hot springs steaming away in the valley and Maisie who likes to play at being Every Girl Her Own Billican, insisted on making tea in one of them. Needless to say it was unspeakable as the springs are full of sulphur. The geysir was better value, it went off just as we were beginning to despair of it, a sweet little thing so slim and girlish, the girls devised a game of throwing a tin cup on to it, the jet of steam works like a catapult and you should have heard how Miss Greenhalge laughed. She laughs conscientiously and seismically. She is very large, very red, and bespectacled (lenses as thick as beer-bottles). The girls among themselves call her La Paloma, you know how romantic they are in these schools. In Reykjavik I found a letter from a little girl called Elsie comparing me to a whole string of heroines, the first being Lucrezia Borgia and the last being Elizabeth Barrett Browning. So it looks like a week of pussy-talk in the lava-fields. Not that Miss Greenhalge would encourage that sort of thing. On the contrary she believes in making her girls behave like public schoolboys—I mean as public schoolboys behave in Ian Hay or in the Mind of God. She wants to see their stuffing, has been reading the latest Peter Fleming. They are all rather in trepidation about their horses. The guides tell us that the last ladies they took this way fell off their horses and all but refused to get on again. Which is a bad lookout when there is no human habitation for thirty miles or so and no possible means of transport and no food except an occasional bilberry. We met our horses for the first time in the gloaming, real little ducks, 17 in all— 7 for us, 2 for the guides, 3 reserves, 5 pack-horses. Maisie fancies herself quite Melton Mowbray now as she rode her first pony several weeks ago. One of the girls, however, Stella, apparently rides at school and even knows how to jump. She is a flashy little girl and is the only one with real leather riding-boots, not that they will do her any good as in Iceland you keep riding through rivers and you need a good honest Dunlop. I am sorry to say that I come last in point of attire because whereas everyone else has riding-breeches I have only got a pair of hopcloth beach-trousers I bought in the South of France. They are somewhat baggy to squeeze into one's gumboots apart from being claret-coloured but why buy new clothes just for a week's Baden-Powelling? Maisie by the way is sleeping in this tent in pyjamas and was very shocked because I got into my sleeping-bag without undressing. To see Maisie struggling out of her undies in two square foot of space makes you realize what built the British Empire. She has been reproving me incidentally for mine—not my Empire, my undies—she says that to wear crêpe-de-chine panties may be all right for Metro-Goldwyn-Mayer but it won't do round the Langjökull. But then Maisie, who is a shirt-and-tie girl herself, is all for the approximation of the sexes; she says that to emphasise one's femaleness is a relic of barbarism like men wearing beards, and that if I do nothing else on this trip it is essential that I shall reduce my bust measurement. Which reminds me that the landscape to-day was rather nice from our bus, at one point there was a perfectly lovely vista all in stratas—first brilliant green grass, almost emerald, then a bank of pink clouds I suppose of dust, then blue serrated crags, and last but not least a glacier floating in the distance, milky-blue—you could hardly believe it was real. But what worries me is that they have no goats. Plenty of fine fat sheep and very clean compared with English ones, but ne'er a goat not even of the littlest. It is like the Irish over cheese. I firmly believe that if the I.F.S. would only (a) make cheese and (b) eat it, they would (a) improve their budget and (b) modify their characters—become more pacific like the

Dutch. Q.E.D. and what was all the fuss about? M. says she is tired of holding the candle so will write you more to-morrow, darling, provided I've not broken my collar-bone. Sweet dreams in the Dolomites.

August 18*th*

Darling, *darling*, DARLING, it is very lucky your poor friend Hetty is alive. The worst night I have had since Aunt Evelyn walked in her sleep—you remember, the fire-extinguisher business. I had great difficulty to start with getting to sleep. For why? (1) Because we had pitched the tent with our heads running downhill, (2) because we had pitched it on bilberry bushes, which kept prickling me through the groundsheet, (3) because Maisie *would* get more and more foetal, so that in the end her feet were playing an absolute barrage on my tummy. All things, however, are possible and I did get to sleep in the end only to be woken by a clammy thing on my face like some very unpleasant beauty treatment—you know when they plaster you with eggs and whey and things—which turned out to be the tent or more precisely the inner cover of the tent because there are two. There was a frightful noise of rain outside and the whole tent was caving in under it, Maisie was swearing and saying she was going down with all hands. I took the ostrich's course and hid my head in my sleeping-bag. Not that that was unduly dry and the foot-end of it was sopping because that was where the door of the tent came. When I popped out my head again, the tent had become very much smaller (Heaven knows it was small enough to start with) and was closing in on us like something in Edgar Allan Poe. So I cowered round the pole in the middle and Maisie and I got entangled like a pair of wet tennis-shoes when one packs them in a hurry. And the rain fell 40 days and 40 nights. Or so it seemed. And the tent got smaller and smaller.

For once in my life I was glad to get up at six—that's what you do on these expeditions. The rain had stopped but the air was full of waterfall. M. and I were very angry to learn that all the others had had a dry night and we made a surly breakfast in our oilskins, M. precariously cooking some coffee on her rather undependable stove. By the time breakfast was over there was actually some sun, in fact the day looked promising. There was much complication over the packing of the food panniers because when a pony carries a pannier each side they have to be exactly the same weight. It sounds easy but it isn't—who knows the relative weights of cheese and hardfiskur? While the others were taking a morning look at the rainbow spray of Gullfoss Maisie and I had our first lapse from esprit de corps and sneaked into the little tin house which caters for trippers where we had some very good coffee. After all there won't be anywhere to buy anything for a week. Then we sorted our horses, Maisie taking the best, a sturdy white beast with solid pillar-like legs (Ranelagh standards don't go here) and off we started. Off we started indeed, bang up the side of the valley; if you have never been on a horse before it does seem a little hard to start on the perpendicular. *I was scared stiff.* And when we got to the top they started trotting—simply terrifying and very very painful —I think my horse must do what is called a brock which even the professionals don't like. In any case their trot is too short for one to do any rising in one's saddle so we had to ride like the cavalry (*sic*) and I fully sympathised with Mary who kept telling the barren plateau that her legs were on fire in tones of bravado mingled with abject panic. We had a respite however when the pack-horses got lost. There is one very naughty white pack-horse who thought he would go home to Geysir where he came from and turning to the left at a fork went flat out for home before anyone realised what was happening. So the two

guides and Maisie and Ruth and Anne followed him while
the rest of us loitered along the right road at a walk and
comparatively painlessly. In single file most of the time,
the road being a mere track through stony deserts rather
reminiscent of Hollywood. The day opened out and there
were highly spectacular views on the left, intense blue
amethyst mountains castellating the glacier. There ought
to be another glacier on the right but we couldn't see it.
Eventually the others came back with the pack-horses
and about 1.0 we stopped for a rest at one of the rare
patches of grass, taking off the horses' saddles and packs
and I expected some food but it seems that that isn't done.
Stella showed off a little by quite superfluously adjusting
her horse's bit while the rest of us creakingly lowered ourselves on to the welcome turf. But very very shortly we
started again and this time we did some cantering. Cantering is even more perilous but not so painful as trotting.
Miss Greenhalge was riding a heavy black pony looking
rather like something in a pantomime; you felt that *she*
might just as well do the walking and the pony trot
between her legs. She (Miss G.) is really very large indeed.
(Maisie says that it is psychological being so tall and that
tall people are running away from life. Hence, at the other
end, Napoleon.) Well, gradually we came up to the hills on
the left which flank the glacier and having passed a snappy
little picture-postcard gorge we encamped about 5.0 on a
spongy piece of grass where we hobbled our horses according to the guides' instructions (the guides are exceedingly
nice not to say long-suffering), turned them adrift and
began putting up our tents. It was then that Maisie and I
made a scientific discovery. This tent of Maisie's has an
outside cover and an inside cover. Well it seems that if
you don't want to get wet you mustn't let these two touch.
Now last night we went out of our way to peg them down
absolutely flush. It seemed so much neater but that was why

we got so wet. The tent is still pretty clammy by the way. Having put up the tents we ate a large meal. The girls are getting hungry and were quite willing to try the despised smoked mutton. Smoked, not cooked mind you; you put your teeth in a hunk and then haul away the hunk in both fists. After that Greenhalge took some of the girls up Bláfell, which is a craggy mountain on the left, while M. and I diverted ourselves more according to our years, stumping through a marsh on the right of our camp in order to inspect the gorge of the river Hvitá. The gorge like all Icelandic gorges is perpendicular and composed of that beastly breaking stone. The Hvitá was turbulent and a most peculiar colour. 'The putty-coloured gletcher,' Maisie said appreciatively. We amused ourselves rolling down stones into it while Maisie told me that her next novel is to deal with the English colony in Fréjus. As we picked our way back through the marsh we kept hearing a single desolate creaking sound—like a creaking gate as M. said—which it turns out is a plover. This land would really make a very good setting for Hell, it reminds me of Gustave Doré's illustrations to the Inferno.   The sphagnum moss everywhere gives the effect of ruins and you can imagine the souls of wicked philosophers sitting here and there on the sharp stones, their beards covered with lichen repenting their false premisses. We got back before the others, so had to make the coffee or rather the coffee and cocoa as Ruth can't drink coffee. M.'s petrol stove is not all it might be and has to be pumped all the time. Greenhalge and the girls came back from Bláfell, they hadn't reached the top of course and what they had was very hard going, all loose shale and stuff—every three foot forward they slipped two foot back. We opened another tin of mutton and found it much better than last night's; we think it has benefited from its jolting on horseback. After dinner Greenhalge opened a little case and, to Maisie's horror, began to offer the girls quinine pills and vegetable laxatives. Maisie has a bee in her bonnet about laxatives; she thinks her inside knows best. I was thirsty after all the mutton and went to the stream for water—it is so cold that it seems to lacerate your gums. Greenhalge is a good sort really, always ready to lend you a knife or a cup and she does all the washing up. The girls don't do anything much in that line excepting possibly Anne who is going to be house-prefect next term. Anne is the best-looking though she will be better looking when she has learned not to pout. She probably has a nice little temper on occasions and does a power of grumbling. Her intonation and vowel sounds are just what you expect from a nice British schoolgirl. Ruth, I should say, is the most intelligent. She says hardly anything but is obviously terribly noticing and puts herself out for nobody. She has just got five credits in the School Certificate and ought to go far. Stella, who as I said is the horsewoman of the party, is conceited but perhaps a little pathetic. She talks a great deal with a lot of wasted emphasis, wears a vulgar but no doubt expensive bracelet, and altogether gives the effect of a cheeky terrier pup that has not been quite properly trained. Mary is an odd girl, neurotic, and capable of quite astonishing ineptitude. She puts questions to Greenhalge like an irrepressible child—'Why are the mountains that shape, Miss Greenhalge?' 'How many kilometres are there in a mile, Miss Greenhalge?' and so on and so on indefinitely. She has a tight little mouth, at least she makes it tight through nervousness, which is rather incongruous with her figure, for she is a strapping wench and would look all right if she could stop putting her hands to her face and get the doleful expression out of her eyes. She has a nice nature and thanks one even superfluously when one does anything for her. She seems to enjoy herself in spite of her fear of the horses and gives

vent to her enjoyment with a quaint mouse-like heartiness.
She shares the large tent with Greenhalge and Anne while
Stella and Ruth have the little tent. Talking of tents
Maisie and I are much more comfortable this evening and
I have invented a scheme for the candle which would do
credit to a Girl Guide. Perfectly simple: you take an ordinary country shoe which laces up, insert the candle in the
laced part, and fasten it there tightly. The shoe is Maisie's.
Maisie says that this tent inside by candlelight looks like
a Stratford-on-Avon set for Julius Caesar. Maisie is smoking like a tramp-steamer. I tell her she is one of those
people like Midas; everything she touches turns to
cigarettes. I have been explaining to her that she will feel
the effects of it in ten years' time when she is forty. She in
her turn has been lecturing me on marriage. She is afraid
that I will become servile. I tell her that Robin is much
too vague for anyone to be servile to him but she maintains that that makes him all the more dangerous and that
I shall have to spend my time running after him with his
season ticket. M. says only unintelligent women ought to
get married. She would prefer me to have a career like
yours, darling, but she forgets I am not qualified. Not that
personally I could breathe if I lived in Cambridge. All
those coffee-parties you have with people talking about
Marx. *And the intrigues, darling, the intrigues!* No, it's
marriage for me unless Robin thinks better of it. I
shouldn't blame him, poor dear, but I don't think he will.
It's curious one should attract people when one isn't
really very attractive. How do you explain it? I really
must go to sleep now, I feel a heroic stiffness in my joints
and it seems highly doubtful whether I shall be able to
mount a horse to-morrow. Maisie seems to be asleep with
a cigarette in her mouth. Her pneumatic bed is sighing
like something out of A. E. Housman. I shouldn't be surprised if it's flat by to-morrow. Good-night, darling.

August 19*th*

To-day started rottenly but was a good day afterwards. We had to pull down our tents and breakfast in icy rain. I had brought no gloves and felt my fingers were going to fall off. The girls looked none too happy though we didn't actually have any tears. We decided that we should all change horses from yesterday and that each day we should take them in rotation in order of age. This meant that I got the one Maisie had yesterday, which is the star horse and goes like the wind. It is pure white all over though Stella says it is technically a grey. But if you call a white horse grey, what do you call a grey horse? Anyhow this horse was a goer and for the first time I felt the joys of horsemanship, though to start with I was very much alarmed especially when it opened its throttle on the edge of a precipice. We had one terrific gallop (canter actually) down a long hill and across a plain of ashes, a dust-storm whipping our faces so that we were riding blind. I turned my face to the left to avoid the grit in my eyes and there saw suddenly a shining sea tilted obliquely upwards, catching the sun. Like something in the Ancient and Modern hymnbook. First I thought it was water and could not understand why it stayed put. It was the icefield. I liked it exceedingly. About mid-day we stopped for a rest and Greenhalge doled out chocolate—four tiny squares per head. I could hardly prevent myself asking for more; it is most instructive to note one's mental unadaptability, one just can't imagine there won't be a shop further on where one can buy all the chocolate one wants. As a matter of fact the next place we came to, Hvitanes, *was* very civilised. It is where I am writing now—in a very swish hut of corrugated iron buttressed all along the sides with growing turf and the walls lined inside with match-boarding. Near by is a little tin house with a man in it whom you pay one króna for your night's lodging and he

sells you cigarettes. We arrived at this blissful spot about
2.0 and after a cold meal were marshalled once more on
horses to go and see the glacier which runs down the
mountain opposite into an attractive lake called Hvitavatn. Unfortunately I did not have the white horse again
but one of the reserves or pack-horses and a very dim
beast he was and needed a deal of slapping. We had an
amazing trek across the flat grassland to the north of the
lake which is nothing but a delta of broad, rapid, and ice-
cold rivers. We had to ford them one after another and
how the horses stand it I can't imagine. Anne and I had
the worst horses and were left a long way behind flounder-
ing ignominiously and hoping the horses wouldn't fall
down with us. Following a devious route we crossed our
last river (about the ninety-ninth) and left the horses on
the further bank under a steep cliff of shale. Which same
we began to climb and clambering up that sort of thing
in gumboots is, I may tell you, no Sunday-school treat.
What was more, we had no idea why we were going up it.
The guide can't talk English, you see. Well, why we were
going up it was in order to have a close-up of the glacier
but glaciers have very bad complexions, and for myself
I would much rather see them from a distance. Greenhalge, Ruth, and I occupied ourselves by climbing a little
conical hill to get a wider view of the countryside which
was certainly very beautiful. We also saw a bit of ice fall
off the edge of the glacier. On our ride home we saw about
thirty young horses running through the grassland at
their pleasure. Where ignorance is bliss ... Little do they
know that in a future season they will have to carry
people like us about. On arriving at our hut Maisie at once
began to cook dinner. She said it was quite time we had a
hot meal so she poked about the hut and our luck was in,
for what did she find but a primus stove and a large pan.
So Maisie put the whole contents of one of the tins of

mutton in the pan and mixed it (against my advice) with water and boiled it on the stove. Oddly enough the result was very good. I bought some more cigarettes from the man in the hut who seemed a little amused by us all. Perhaps they don't know their Angela Brazil round here. I notice that the Icelanders in spite of their tough existence have a certain whimsicality not common among the other Scandinavians. Perhaps the explanation is that given by an Icelander in Reykjavik—that it's the Irish in them which accounts for this. After dinner every girl washed her own dish but I not having a dish merely rinsed the grease from my hands in the broad and serene river that flows between the hut and the mountains. I should mention that a little further down this river is the most exquisite convenience, a kind of wooden sentry-box which projects over the water; I have already visited it twice; in this barren country such comfort is really lyrical. After washing up we wrote our names in the Visitors' Book and all of us except the guides played rummy by the light of an oil-lamp (unheard-of luxury!) in which Ruth had all the luck, sitting there saying nothing, with a pale quiet smile, time after time laying down her cards and going out. Irritating little girl! Not so irritating as Stella though, who talked without ceasing. The room got in the most awful fug as Greenhalge had allowed the girls to smoke (give a pawn and take a queen, you know; Greenhalge is all for making men of them) which is all right for them because they are sleeping upstairs (fancy having an upstairs!) but not so good for Maisie and me who are having this room to ourselves. I have just been outside for a breath of fresh air and saw the huge mountain opposite floating on nothing—the nothing was of course ice. There is some talk of another party whom we may meet on this route—N.U.S. I think—gloomy how educational the place seems to be becoming. I am not sure that I like the English in Iceland. The ones coming over on my boat were a very odd lot. The second class much nicer than the first. There was a little cockney confectioner who did tricks with his false teeth and was reading a book on how to be a successful writer. Then there were two Welsh Jews from Birkenhead who had a great many odd bits of curious knowledge and one of them used to sing The Rose of Tralee and Die Lorelei; fruity wasn't the word for it. There was a young tax-collector from Preston who carried the Oxford Book of English Verse in his pocket. And there were half a dozen old schoolmistresses (but they travelled first) from Manchester who had already gone the pace in Finland and Russia and Brussels. I wonder what they all want out of Iceland. Or just to say they have been there? My bed to-night is on a wooden bench with a mattress under my sleeping-bag. It being comparatively warm, I am sleeping in my panties and vest. I will now try if I can blow out the oil-lamp without getting up for it.

August 20th

Darling, I am nearly dead. Up at six again to-day and my horse was a demon. And that wicked Maisie who had it yesterday, never let on about it. It has the brock all right. When we started this morning the trouble began with its saddle slithering down under its tummy. These horses have a deplorable habit of inflating themselves when you fasten their girths. Well by the time I had tightened its girth I had to catch up the others, so first I trotted and then I cantered and really I don't know which was the more uncomfortable. Well, when we did catch up the others, my malicious beast charged straight in among the pack-horses and gored my leg against one of the wooden panniers. And after that it ran away with me, tossing me sky-high in its cantering so that I had to hang on by the mane and my eyes were streaming with the

wind in them. 'If I don't fall off this horse,' I said, 'I shall
be very proud of myself.' That finished it. We were then
riding along a narrow track sunk in the ground to a depth
of three feet or more—the sort of place you ought to proceed at a walk but where my horse suddenly decided to go
full speed ahead so that my right foot caught in the right
bank of the track and I fell gracefully over its tail with
my foot still in the stirrup. I will say that the horse stood
still till I disintricated myself. After that we got among
rocks and there we all just had to walk. On our left was a
river in a very narrow gorge, the sort you could jump over
if you were a fool, and the sides moulded into all sorts of
elegant concaves. The mountains beyond it licked down
great tongues of ice and it would all have been very
romantic if I had not felt so sore. We stopped for our mid-
day snack in a pleasant meadow encircled by mountains
and sitting in the shelter of a bank by a little stream ate
smoked mutton and raisins. Maisie, who fancies herself
with a camera, went round taking art shots of people
through each other's legs. I must say we were well worth
photographing. The cold weather makes us all look much
funnier in our various defences against it. Maisie herself
has taken to wearing a sou'-wester with an old felt hat
fastened on over it with a safety-pin. Her sou'wester is
bright yellow, her oilskin coat is black, and her enormous
gumboots are brown. Wisps of hair straggle down over her
forehead and when she walks she moves like something
that is more at home in the water. Margery Greenhalge
also looks pretty odd. She wears an amazing woollen
helmet with earflaps which combined with her goggles and
general outsizeness makes her look like a piece of Archaic
Greek sculptury. Stella, goodness knows why, appears to
be wearing a blue and white bathing-cap. Anne has a kind
of a Cossack hat which would suit her as an equestrienne
for Bertram Mills. After our snack, we took our horses by

the reins and led them up over a very steep and stony
ridge; it is the first time we have done this for as far as they
are concerned they would carry us over a tightrope. At
the top I let the others ride ahead and proceeded at a walk
beside the guides and pack-horses. It was on this occasion
that I thought I saw Greenhalge in the distance and it
turned out to be a cairn. We caught up the advance-guard
in a frightful state of emotion. Anne had cut her finger and
two of the girls were in tears. Greenhalge, redder than
ever, rushed round the pack-horses tearing open all the
panniers for iodine; anyone would have thought the girl
was going to die. Maisie was explaining that you usually
cut your finger because you wanted to—like making
Spoonerisms she said. Anne did her best to be a lovely
martyr but she did not have the whole house with her as
both the guides and little Hetty were definitely bored.
These queens of the schoolroom begin to think that anything will go. The day was now getting misty and the ride
dreary. I held in my beast and trailed along humbly with
the jingling pack-horses, losing the sense of time. I thought
the ride would never come to an end. But it did. Suddenly
we came over a rise and there was a long and shallow
valley, desolate enough for anyone and smoking away like
the dumping-ground of a great city. I thought the whole
valley was on fire but coming closer I saw that the smoke
was trails of steam, dozens of ribbons of steam blowing
from left to right. This was our destination—the hot
springs of Hveravellir. It would now be about teatime,
the others had already left their horses by the hut and
were walking back to look at the springs. 'You *must* see
the hut,' Maisie shouted to me, 'it is just like a henhouse.'
And it *was*, my dear, but only the sort of henhouse you
would find in a depressed area. The walls are of rough
stone banked outside with turf, the corrugated iron roof
is also covered with turf; the stone walls inside are unlined

172

and the whole place is incredibly damp. There is a nasty
platform to sleep on three foot up from the floor and another platform higher up under the roof which you reach
by a ladder. After surveying these apartments I went to
have a look at the springs. A real witches' laundry with the
horizontal trailers of steam blowing through the mist,
some from little pop-holes in the ground and others from
quite large pools, most of them circular. Some of these
latter were lovely, might have been invented by Arthur
Rackham—stone basins of highly coloured water varying
from Reckitt's blue to green, and round the edge yellowish
growths of sulphur. The crust of stone around them seems
only about four inches thick and you expect any moment
to go down like Dathan and Abiram. The water is practically boiling and the whole valley smells of bad eggs.
Hveravellir was where an eighteenth-century robber made
his hide-out for a year; he must have got dreadfully tired
of his sulphuretted drinking-water. We made our coffee
with it and I cannot say I would fancy it every day. But
it does seem a waste that all this hot water should be
bubbling away here for nothing. When you think of all the
trouble housewives are having this very minute with
boilers and how people who still use ranges forget to put
in or pull out the dampers and how every other lodging-
house has a geyser over the bath which won't work properly. Why didn't Nature put Hveravellir in Bayswater?
Greenhalge, Maisie, Anne, and I (being the elect) are sleeping on the upper platform close to the iron roof. The roof
drips water and spiders. This evening was not a great
success. When we opened the food panniers it was found
that the cheese was thickly coated with coffee. Greenhalge,
noble as ever, set to work to decarbonise it (her own
phrase) but we were all discouraged as the cheese is the
one food which anyone would think of eating in England.
After supper we played rummy on the lower platform by

the light of candles in shoes (my little patent, you remember) and a very odd scene we made like a Victorian engraving of a meeting of Old Covenanters. One good mot on this occasion: Greenhalge suddenly said 'O here's a knave with such a sympathetic expression' to which Ruth replied quietly 'Then it must be a queen'. Maisie was frightfully pleased. The Icelandic cards all have different faces, you see, and there's no doubt that our present company see little need for a world of two sexes. They will grow out of that of course. I've seen 'em do it before. Incidentally I haven't noticed much galanterie on the part of the guides. Maisie says it's because the North is ascetic but I think it's just because we're dowdy. The Icelandic girl is never without her lipstick. Your poor Hetty has lost hers in her sleeping-bag. I said to Maisie 'Haven't you got anything of the sort?' and she said 'The only thing that ever goes on *my* face is good honest Lifebuoy Soap'. She has a tablet with her which she takes down to the gletcher. Personally I'm giving up ablutions; when I get home I shall go to Elizabeth Arden's. Good-night, darling. Perhaps you're sleeping in a hut too. Mountaineers always do, don't they? Maisie has been telling me terrible things about mountaineers and I think you had better be careful with your new friend. What a life you have, don't you! But with all that choice you ought to hit it off some day. Good-night.

August 21st

I had to get up in the night—I think it was the sulphuretted coffee. Or rather I should say get down because there I was up on the platform absolutely wedged in with corpses. So instead of going down by the ladder I did a little exhibition of gym and swung myself down by my hands, nearly falling over a guide. It *was* unpleasant outside, a thick Scotch mist and the ground very cold under my stockinged feet. Of course I oughtn't really to be wearing my six-and-elevens from Marshall and Snelgrove out here but I never thought of bringing anything woollen. One can't think of everything after all. Maisie says she is going to write to Robin about me. Robin wouldn't know though; it is the sort of thing he does himself. I felt definitely ill when I got back to bed and kept wondering whether I had caught a disease from my sleeping-bag or whether it was just that nasty horse yesterday. But I will spare you the details of my symptoms. I woke up at 6.0 with a dream-couplet running in my head. Until I was properly awake I thought it was terribly good. It went like this:

> 'We write no ethics down the cabin walls,
> There are ethics at home at all.'

I wonder would the Surrealists pay me anything for that. To-day we did our longest trek—70 kilometres. You work that out in miles and take off your hat to us! And what was more, we walked half of it on our own feet. Because to-day we were doing undiscovered country. Doesn't that excite you, darling? We had to get across, you see, from Hveravellir to Arnarvatn. Well, people don't do that direct. They go up much farther north and then down again. But we hadn't time for that because the girls have to catch a boat. The guides themselves were quite excited and amused themselves by building cairns—a game to which the country is admirably adapted. In the centre of Iceland there are only three kinds of scenery—Stones, More Stones, and All Stones. The third type predominated to-day. The stones are the wrong size, the wrong shape, the wrong colour, and too many of them. They are not big enough to impress and not small enough to negotiate. Absolutely unpicturesque and absolutely non-utilitarian. We stumbled over their points in gumboots, dragging the wretched horses behind us. And at the same time we were climbing. Maisie was disgusted. She said it was like after a party which no one had tidied up. It's certainly hard to think how a country gets in a mess like this. A geologist would know, I suppose. The glacier was now to our south and looking distinctly jaded. There were peaky mountains on our right, dull and sullen in the mist. About 1.0 we found a fallen-in cave, a thing like a subway and no more beautiful, and stopped there to eat chocolate. Ruth too seems to be suffering from the sulphur. Then we went on again over the stones. Next time we ford a river I shall be very surprised if our boots do not turn out to be punctured. I tried to remember my T. S. Eliot and said something to Maisie about stony rubbish and dry bones but Maisie said anyone would be an optimist who expected to find anything as human as a dry bone in these parts. Then we came to the dry bed of a river which seemed even more desolate still and was also a litter of stones. And then at long last we came to a miracle—a small patch of grass with sheep on it. Not that I would be those sheep all the same. Still they seem to thrive on it. In fact, the sheep in Iceland all look the size of horses. Once we had seen the sheep things went better. The sun even came out. We came to a clear stream where the horses could drink and not long after that we reached our destination—a very beautiful lake lined with long gleams of silver in the low sun. Here we found our third hut—far more primitive than even the last one and a great deal smaller. Maisie and I commandeered it on the ground that we are the least well equipped in the way of tents. I think we made a mistake. Not that it hasn't an admirable situation. It stands over a little river which falls in a cascade to the lake; it is called the Skammá or Short River and is rapturously cold to drink. Away to the south-east stands the Eiriksjökull, a dark, square, upstanding mass of mountain with white flaps of ice coming down over its walls. But it is built of turf and stone—the hut, I mean—and the turf is falling out of the walls and roof and the sleeping-plat-

form was thick with earth and cobwebs and Maisie began
by putting her foot through it. There is also a very peculiar
smell. We prepared for a meal outside the hut and Maisie
on opening the pack which contains her stove found that
it had fallen irrevocably to pieces. The fruit of our long
trek. Well, that was that—no coffee or cocoa and we had
to drink the Skammá. So then we tried to think of something original to do and we played rummy in the hut.
There was so little room when the girls all got on the platform that we had to stick the candles on the crossbeam.
Every now and again a sod of turf would fall on us from
the roof and tempers were none too good. The girls said
they were jolly glad they were sleeping in their tents.
Various people have written their names on the beams of
this hut, including one F. J. Smith, who adds sympatheti-
cally 'Very cold'. The hut boasts one teacup with a design
of pink roses and tied up with string. Maisie and I have
been discussing what can cause the smell under our bed.
Maisie was very pleased this evening because Stella broke
her bracelet. She broke it in a typical manner by snapping
it backwards and forwards. Maisie says all those orna-
ments are relics of barbarism and that both men and
women nowadays should aim at dressing in uniforms. No
frills and no bright colours. That is civilisation, Maisie
says. A sweet-tooth is a bad sign too, she thinks, like the
Icelanders sugaring their potatoes. I tend to agree here.
I think I had now better put out the remaining candle as
it is leaning sideways and plastering Maisie's shoe with
wax. Her shoes are having a hard time as they are also used
for ashtrays. This black hole of a hut has rather a roué
appearance at the moment as Maisie has hung her bras-
sière from the crossbeam. It is deplorably cold and the
wooden platform is hard under my sleeping-bag. I thought
very hard and managed to remember a Latin quotation—
probitas laudatus et alget—which means roughly that it is

a fine thing to be a Girl Guide but that you can't keep
warm in kudos. How only too true, darling. 'Never again'
Maisie and I have been saying to each other. Well, here
goes the light.

August 22nd

I woke at 6.0 feeling half frozen. Maisie in spite of
her pneumatic mattress, sleeping-bag and extra blankets
maintained that she was even colder. Rain came on at
breakfast time blown by a cold wind off the Langjökull.
After breakfast walking fifty yards up the Skammá I came
upon a rock adorned with a hammer and sickle in red
paint. It was like Robinson Crusoe seeing a human foot-
print. The rain became definitely vehement so we prepared
ourselves for a bad day. I put on puttees over my beach-
trousers and borrowed some gloves from Anne. Then we
clambered into our already sopping saddles and set off
leaning into the wind and trying to cover our knees with
our oilskins. What a morning! As we moved south and
drew level with the Eiriksjökull the wind increased,
whipping straight across the glacier and nearly blowing us
off our horses. The rain became hail. When we dismounted
to give our horses a rest we realised how wet we were about
the knees. Greenhalge remarked that when roughing it in
this way it is always a good thing to think of the discom-
forts of the people climbing Everest. Maisie says she
would rather think about the people dining at the Ritz.
Maisie was looking odder than ever to-day as she had for
the first time put on her yellow oilskin leggings. She began
by wearing them inside her gumboots but after half-an-
hour or so realised that the water was collecting round her
feet so she put them on over her boots which no doubt
served a purpose but no one could call it very chic. She
looked as if she had webbed feet. Well, on and on we rode
through the stinging rain; it was so nasty it was really

rather enjoyable. And we all felt rather heroic, I think. I
heard two of the girls telling each other what a lot of grit
La Paloma has. La Paloma, you remember, is Miss Greenhalge. We came to a very nice round pool lying flat in
the rocks which the wind was whipping up into ostrich
feathers. What really kept us going however was the
knowledge that to-night we should spend for the first time
in a human habitation, an outpost farm at a place called
Kalmanstunga. You have no idea what a difference it
makes knowing that you won't have to bother with tents.
As for huts the less said about last night's hut the better.
In the afternoon the rain gradually subsided and stopping
our horses on the brink of a yawning cave we climbed
down into the shelter of its mouth and there ate our four
portions of chocolate. It then transpired that the chief
guide was for some unknown reason very anxious to do us
the honours of the cave and lead us underground to another opening goodness knows how far distant. Wishing
to be polite we agreed to this and our first impetus had
carried us well into the darkness before we realised that to
play this game with any success whatsoever you need a
candle per head. Greenhalge, reliable as ever, produced a
candle but one candle is inadequate for eight persons, and
I thought we were due for a serious accident for in all
directions you could hear people and rocks falling over
each other. It was not a very handsome cave, what one
could see of it, and the floor was entirely covered with a
jumble of large rocks so that you could only make a yard
of progress by climbing say six foot up and four foot down
again. And one should not do these things in long oilskin
coats. Our one candle did not promise to last and the girls,
Anne in particular, became a trifle agitated so we explained to the guide, rather to his chagrin, that we would
now go back again. The one attractive thing about this
cave was the ice which grew in it, sprouting upwards in

shapes like empty champagne bottles, each with a nice
round hole in the top of the neck. I broke one of these
bottle-necks off and sucked it on our return journey. It
was deliciously refreshing. Poor Maisie had a rough passage, she kept falling over the flaps of her leggings and I
was afraid she would break something. We all, however,
emerged to the light without injury. The rain had now
stopped and our clothes were again comparatively dry.
After an hour or so we came to an unwonted sight—a gate.
The first gate we had seen since Gullfoss. Admittedly it
was a rather tenuous gate precariously suspended in a
barely existent-fence. All the same it was a gate and a
symbol of civilisation. The going was better now and we
trotted happily for Kalmanstunga. We got there about
6.0, coming to it down a steep hill. Maisie had ridden ahead,
announced our arrival and ordered coffee. The farmhouse
is a large respectable building of corrugated iron standing
in the middle of an emerald green tún. Tún (pronounced
toon) is the specially cultivated meadow attached to an
Icelandic farm. Kalmanstunga has many stone outhouses
roofed with nice green sods; this kind of roof always has
a Beatrix Potter look about it. Having got off my horse
and splashed through the little stream separating the
stables from the house I arrived in time to hear Greenhalge
make the following remark—that it was a really astonishing thing in such a position to find a farmhouse of corrugated iron where one would expect a thatched cottage
covered with wisteria. Personally I didn't care what it was
covered with provided I got my hot coffee. Yesterday,
remember, we had nothing but cold water. The house was
already full of people, being the only house for miles and
in a strategic position for travellers. We were waited on,
in fact, by a fellow-guest, an Icelandic lady who had spent
most of her life in Denmark, Scotland, and London. She
was a non-stop talker but an efficient waitress, put two

tables together for us and laid them with a wonderful meal of coffee and cakes. Marie Antoinette's economic suggestion, 'If they have no bread, give them cake', would be a perfectly sound one in Iceland for the Icelanders are the world's greatest cake-eaters. In many of the farms they eat them at every meal starting with breakfast. When we had put down all we could the talkative lady cleared away and in the course of an enthusiastic statement of her love for Britain told us that dinner would be ready in half-an-hour. So for half an hour Maisie played the piano—it is very unusual to have a piano and not a harmonium—and then dinner arrived and our fears of a sweet soup were not fulfilled. The Icelanders when they want to give you a special treat put brilliantine in their soup or else flavour it perniciously with almond. Hot almond is not a good taste. The only thing to do with these soups is to drown them in stewed rhubarb which they tend to give you at the same time. Maisie says that Icelandic cooking makes her think of a little boy who has got loose with Mother's medicine-chest. After dinner we were shown our rooms— two rooms leading out of each other, very cosy and hospitable but with rather a shortage of beds. The four girls are sharing two small beds in the first room and in the second room are two beds which have been run together. Greenhalge naturally has one and Maisie and I are sharing the other. All the beds here are furnished with deckers, if you spell it like that, and as a decker can't be tucked in it is not ideal for covering two well-grown females such as Maisie and myself. Maisie is elbowing me inconsiderately so you must forgive my writing. I can quite clearly hear the girls whispering next door. Presumably they don't realise we can hear them. The two nearest to us are talking about La Paloma (La P. herself can't hear, I think, as she is the far side of us and seems to be already asleep). One of the two girls says that La Paloma has a very beautiful

181

smile but the other says that it is not such a spiritual
smile as one Miss Robinson's. Now they have got on to
me. They do not think my smile is nice; one of them says
it is cynical and the other says I use make-up (this is not
at the moment true as I have lost my lipstick). Now they
have reverted to La Paloma and are wondering if she
meant either of them when she said to-day, 'Some girls grow
up much quicker than others.' One of them says that
Miss Robinson gave her a brooch at the end of last term—
one of those too sweet little brooches with fox-terriers on
them. The other refuses to believe this; they are both
getting piqued. Now the other—I mean the one—has got
out of bed to look for the brooch in her rucksack. She has
found it and is showing it off in triumph. The other is
distinctly huffy, she will not believe that it came from
Miss Robinson but says that the one bought it herself in
Woolworth's. The one answers indignantly that you can
see brooches like that in Bond Street. Now the other
starts a hare; she says that *she* had a Christmas card from
Miss Robinson last Christmas. The one is rather stumped
over this but rallies and says in a sinister tone, 'Last
Christmas was last Christmas.' Now there is going to be a
scrap. No, there was no scrap; they merely had a general
post and everyone changed beds. Maisie says there is
nothing new under the sun. Good-night, darling.

August 23rd

To-day began in comfort and ended in misery. We got
up for once at a rational hour and even had a little hot
water to sponge our faces with. While we were dressing
that extraordinary girl Mary had an attack of music. She
gave a quite remarkably tuneless rendering of 'O God our
help in ages past'. And when someone ironically congratu-
lated her she said, 'Yes and I'm also very fond of Jerusalem
the Golden.' Breakfast was at 9.0 and lunch at 10.0. We

said, 'Isn't that a little soon for lunch?' but they explained
that it was quite all right because they kept their clocks
two hours ahead of Reykjavik. Anyway lunch was a thun-
dering meal—mutton drowned in gravy followed by a
mix-up of fruit and sago. Overnight our clothes had been
considerately dried and we now put on our numerous
extras although the morning looked fine and mild. Our
caution was justified. The guides kept us waiting while
they went over the horses' shoes and we stood outside the
farm looking over to the Langjökull. They say that to
cross the Langjökull here from Hvitavatn takes 13—or
is it 16—hours. That is one thing we will *not* do though
I am sure Greenhalge would have great fun rescuing the
girls from crevasses. Greenhalge once went on a visit to a
mission school in India where she heroically killed a
scorpion. There was such a nice dog who talked to us
while we were waiting, a sort of little sheepdog, black and
white with a thick but not very long coat, a broad forehead
and a spitzy foreface. Nearly all Icelandic dogs are of this
type except that the colour varies. They are amazingly
friendly creatures; it is considered a bad trait in an Icelandic dog if he barks at strangers. They tend to be called
Gosi which is the name of the knave in an Icelandic pack
of cards. I must bring you home some Icelandic cards; the
kings and queens are figures from the sagas and the aces
are waterfalls. Badly drawn but a less expensive souvenir
than a sheepskin or a silver fox. Iceland is a barren land
for souvenirs. Of course one can always bring home little
bits of lava for one's friends—I saw the Manchester school-
teachers doing this at the Great Geysir—but I am afraid
I have the wrong sort of friends. Maisie and I had a conversation this morning about the foreignness of Iceland.
We decided that not counting the scenery, which is of
course unthinkable, there are only two really foreign
things in the place—(1) the system of nomenclature and

(2), as already mentioned, the food. The former is just lunatic; in order to use a telephone directory you have to know everyone's christian names and then you are not much farther because all their christian names are the same. The people themselves are not nearly so foreign as the Irish or the yokels of Somerset. You can't imagine any of them behaving like the people in the sagas, saying 'That was an ill word' and shooting the other man dead. Disappointing, still one needn't travel if one wants to see odd behaviour. You are wonderfully situated, of course, in Cambridge. Talking of local colour did I tell you about the ship's electrician I met on the Flying Scot? He told me that Abyssinia was largely inhabited by black Jews with ginger hair. But to get on with my record. The guides finished tinkering with the horses and we set off gaily in the brisk and lively morning. They all waved us off from the farm. It would be rather nice to spend the winter at one of these farms—a terrific fug, constant jabber on the radio, ivy growing in pots and the family reading Hall Caine. It was sad to think there would be no farm to-night. But the reality was worse than our expectations. We began by fording a turbulent river, the water came over the tops of our boots—at least of our left boots—the girls thought it was a scream. It's not such a scream though to have water in your boots for hours afterwards. The Icelandic pony is of course an amphibian. He can even swim a river with someone in the saddle but it has to be the right someone. There is a legend of an Icelander who in the early days of tobacco used to swim his horse two miles out to sea to meet the tobacco boat. After fording the river the rain started, a drizzle but very unpleasant. One could not decide whether to fasten up the collar of one's oilskin or not. And then we went through a so-called birch forest —a scrubby little affair about four foot high but it does seem quite companionable after the miles and miles and

miles of no vegetation but moss. A little later we reached
a very nice piece of grassland where Ruth contrived to be
thrown when her pony put its foot in a hole. From Kalmanstunga south we had been following a track which is
used by cars—one of those thick red lines which look so
impressive on the map. Nowhere else in the world I suppose would this be called a road but it is used as such for
we met two buses on it. And as a matter of fact whoever
constructed these roads is a public benefactor even though
constructing consists merely in moving aside the stones,
that is the bigger stones. Our progress to-day was again
stony once we had left the short stretch of grassland. We
got in between Langjökull on the left and a mountain
with the charming name of Ok on the right and once we
had done that all we could think of was getting somewhere
else. But we didn't. We went on and on and the landscape
remained the same. It was like walking the wrong way on
a moving staircase. We were close in under the Langjökull
but it was covered with mist. Maisie was in a frightful
temper. This valley is called Kaldidalur which means Cold
Dale—apt but inadequate. The Icelanders are rather
proud of it as a show-piece of scenery and no doubt on a
clear day it may be quite beautiful if one drives through it
quickly in a car. But all we could see was a thirty-foot
radius of stones. The stones were too much for my horse
and it took to stumbling. We came across the ancient
wreck of a very primitive touring car—more desolate than
the bones of a camel in a film about the Foreign Legion.
The rain never came on very properly but it was con-
tinuously damp and we began to think we preferred
yesterday's weather which at least made us feel heroic.
About supper-time we got down into lower country and
riding on ahead of the guides stopped our horses on a
marshy piece of pasture ground on the edge of a dreary
lake. We hoped this wasn't our destination but it was. It

is called Brunnar. We set up our tents on squelchy ground in the drizzle and owing to the direction of the wind and the lie of the ground M. and I have to sleep with our heads out of the door to-night. However, we have erected across it a barrier of kitbags, gumboots, and canvas panniers. The guides think we are funny because we all look so gloomy. The guides deserve high marks to-night for, after we had eaten a melancholy meal in the rain and were all moaning because, owing to the breakdown of Maisie's stove there was no hot drink to wash it down with, the guides came along rather shyly and asked (mainly by dumb show) if we would like the loan of their stove. We didn't know they had a stove but sure enough they brought along a minute rudimentary object like a small canister which we welcomed with open arms and it actually worked though I must admit it took some time. While we were waiting patiently for our coffee Maisie made a sudden scene and said she would *not* have highly scented foods in her bed. This referred to some cheese and smoked mutton which I had left there. When the coffee arrived we had to drink it not only, as always, without milk but also without sugar. The sugar is kept in an old tobacco tin, and when we opened it to-night every single lump had turned a deep puce colour. Quite inexplicable and rather sinister. No one, even the guides, had the nerve to try any of it. Maisie and I are now lying wedged in our tent hoping for the best. The Icelandic year has passed its prime and the guides are taking no more expeditions after this one. I feel I should mention that we saw some ptarmigan on arriving at Brunnar. You won't know any more about ptarmigan than I do but it is quite time I gave you a nature note (there is *awfully* little nature around here). Maisie and I, clammy and rheumatic, are listening to the schoolgirls chattering in their tents next door and are asking each other whose fault this is. We have told the guides that we want to start early to-morrow. To-morrow brings us to civilisation and there is no point in staying in this particular little swamp a minute longer than we need.

August 24th

Well, here we are in Valhalla—that really is what it is called—the hotel at Thingvellir. Thingvellir is where they used to have the Thing, which was the Icelandic name for parliament and a very good name too, don't you think. It is *the* historic showplace. Not that there is anything to see except geology but it is amusing geology—rifts and such. It would have been nicer if we had had better weather but the day has been damp and misty and Ruth quarrelled with Stella because Stella intrigued with Anne to prevent Mary riding beside Greenhalge. Mary was in tears (she admires Greenhalge intensely across a great gulf of incompatibility) and Ruth demanded back from Stella an Eversharp pencil which she had given her and which Stella refused to return. We were up this morning at 6.0 with no appetite whatsoever and intending to leave Brunnar as quickly as possible. Naturally the ponies chose just this one morning to get lost, the guides disappeared over the horizon in search of them and the rest of us waited in our marsh among our bags and chattels like people in a country railway station in the West of Ireland where the train has stopped on the way to talk to the cows. The tents were packed up, the food panniers strapped down, ourselves muffled in scarves, and Maisie running round taking photos. They will not come out of course but Maisie does not like to waste her time. At long last the horses returned quite unpenitent and off we started. I had an excellent horse to-day, a large black one with a white star on its forehead, and we got our best gallop yet across a long expanse of grey sand by a lake called Sandurvatn. In our heart of hearts I think we were all playing sheikhs.

It is very nice when the sand flies up in your face and you plop up and down in the saddle to a perfectly regular rhythm—chichibu, chichibu, chichibu. It is not really galloping of course, only cantering. Our stampede across the sands went to the head of that old malefactor, the white pack-horse, who broke loose and galloped after us, throwing off Maisie's bed en route. Anne, who has a habit of mock indignation (at least it starts mock and ends serious) was very cross indeed with the white pack-horse and said it should be thoroughly well thrashed; she is soon, as I said, going to be house prefect. Maisie's bed was re-established (we had to gather up various very odd articles which had fallen out of it on the sands, it is by way of also being a hold-all) and we went up slowly over the water-shed, from the top of which we had a fine view of the plain that reaches to Thingvellir, a fine plain that looks a lot more livable than anything we have seen lately. We pastured our horses at the foot of the descent and then went all out for our Mecca, reaching it about 2.0 in the afternoon—a good deal earlier than we had expected. We went straight to the hotel and ordered coffee. The hotel is about the only building here but there is also a minute church. While we were waiting for the guides and pack-horses who had been left a very long way behind, we nearly had a serious mishap thanks to the incredible stupidity of Mary and Stella. Stella, as you remember, is supposed to know about horses. Well those two infant geniuses finding their horses had no hobbles tied them to the two ends of a ladder belonging to the hotel. Inevitable result: the horses ran amok and the ladder suffered from schism. Maisie and I from the breakfast room looked out over the landscape and suddenly saw these two horses catapult across it with the ladders (or half a ladder each I should say) clattering behind them. By some miracle they escaped injury and we said nothing about the ladder at the hotel.

After our coffee Maisie and I, with the unanimous support
of the girls (sloppy little things!) began to work upon
Greenhalge to induce her not to camp out to-night; she
had her eye upon a peculiarly unprepossessing site between
two low-grade ditches. After all what is a tent? A tent is a
make-believe house; when there is a real house about why
go on making a belief one? Greenhalge lowered her standards to a compromise. We had suggested, out of the
cunning of our hearts, that we should all sleep in sleeping-
bags in the dance-hall. This sounded enough like a barracks to appeal to Greenhalge's passion for hardship so
she cried off the tents and said we would all rough it in the
dance-hall. But when we asked the hotel people if we
could rough it in the dance-hall they said unfortunately
no because it was wanted for 250 Frenchmen who are
coming to breakfast to-morrow. So (the virtuous are re-
warded in the end) they have supplied us instead with
little cabins on the ground floor, six foot square, two beds
in each, walls of matchboarding, one krona a night. That
is what I call good value but poor Greenhalge felt she had
been tricked. In the afternoon we walked up the gorge.
Everyone has to walk up the gorge here. Just like when
you go to Tintern Abbey you have to see the moon
through an arch. The gorge is an odd phenomenon and
would be nice for a picnic. The spirit of the sagas descended upon me and I walked through the river in my
gumboots. This was just above the fall and I liked to think
it was dangerous; whether it was dangerous or not I got a
lot of water in my boots and had to hurry home. Maisie,
Ruth, and Mary remained behind and in a spirit of emula-
tion climbed down the waterfall itself; or so they told me
afterwards. I doubted it because they seemed to be quite
dry. When we were all together again in the hotel it was
suggested we should go a nice row on the lake in the mist.
No one showed great enthusiasm for this and we ordered

some coffee instead. M. and I went to our cabin to change
and I quite innocently did a perfect turn à la Brothers
Bronett—you remember, the clowns at Olympia—by
pulling off my boots and thereby flooding out our bedroom. Not only our bedroom because it flowed along the
passage and we could hear it lapping on unknown doors
in the distance. No one would believe so much water could
come out of one pair of gumboots. Maisie was rather cross
about it. We took our clothes to the kitchen to be dried
and sat down to our coffee and cigarettes; we have been
hard up for cigarettes since Kalmanstunga. Here as everywhere else you can only buy Commanders. There are
several oil paintings in this hotel, notably a rather lunatic
picture of the Thingvellir gorge by that curious painter
Kjarval. Kjarval's gorge was not at all as we saw it but
then most of the Icelandic painters seem to see with the
eyes of chameleons. Cascades of paint, a drunk pink sky,
a whole lot of things looking like sunflowers and wheels
flying about over the rocks, a total effect of perfectly
tropical luxuriance. I am not sure however that I do not
prefer this mania for colour to the kind of fake Cézanne
landscape which a few of their painters go in for. There
is also here a very sombre lava-scape by one Johann
Briem which only demonstrates that the Icelandic cubist
has no call to distort as Nature has done that for him. I
have also in this hotel been observing the Icelandic girls.
Fine strapping wenches on the whole, with tilted noses,
figures rather tight and slightly assertive bosoms. Their
expression of face tends to be self-possessed. I should think
there is no fluff in their relationships. We had hardly
finished coffee when we had our evening meal in Greenhalge's cabin. We chose her room because she has it to
herself but all the same I am sorry for her. It is not so nice
to sleep in a room which is stuccoed with food. I haven't
noticed if it applies to myself but I must say the others

have become rather untidy eaters on this expedition. Greenhalge was wonderfully good-humoured about it; perhaps she felt it made up for not sleeping in a tent. After dinner we played a little desultory rummy and when the girls had gone to bed Greenhalge and Maisie had a long and very serious conversation about adolescence, education, and psychology. It all began when Greenhalge said that one of the 'difficult' girls at her school had been sent to a psycho-analyst. This set Maisie off on her hobby-horse. No one, according to M., ought to go to an analyst except of their own free will, i.e. if they are so unhappy that analysis is the only hope for them. Now your 'difficult' girls, as Maisie quite rightly maintains, are probably no more unhappy than anyone else; it is only that they get in the way of the headmistress. The headmistress wants everything to be right and tight in her own little hive and doesn't care a hang for the girls' lives as individuals. So off they go to the analyst who removes their difficulties and from then on they are as clean and harmless about the house as a neuter cat. (Maisie's comparison, not mine.) All very well for the house but what about the cat, says Maisie. Maisie says it is a bad thing in Freud that he always suggests that neurosis is something to be got rid of. On the contrary, says M., all the progress in this world is due to neurosis. If Sylvia Pankhurst had been analysed in her 'teens, we shouldn't have women's suffrage. Let us have as much neurosis as we can stand. This reminded me of an argument I had with Robin, which I now repeated to Maisie. M. says I must tell Robin I refuse to have children if he is going to Truby King them. I must only have them on condition that they are to be exposed to germs, allowed to retain their neuroses and never on any account given purges. From purges we got on to religion and we all agreed that poor old Freud is sadly off the rails in *The Future of an Illusion*. All that stuff about the pure and

191

scintillating mind of the child being blunted and crippled
by its early religious instruction. Not that *I* am any advo-
cate for religious instruction, which is one of the reasons
I like Iceland. Iceland is one of the few places where you
don't feel it in the air when it's Sunday. I dare say though
that the introduction of Christianity did indirectly pro-
mote the amelioration of social conditions (just to show
you I can write like a don too) for the life of the sagas was
not quite what we call civilised. Talking of civilisation it
is comfortable in this bed and I very much hope to-morrow
night Greenhalge doesn't force us to camp out at Laugarvatn. She was saying sadly to-night that the expedition
had really been very easy. No really gruelling tests of
the girls' endurance. Judging by the girls' behaviour at
Kaldidalur I should say this was just as well. How do you
find your endurance in the Dolomites? Good-night, darling.
To-morrow is our last trek.

August 25th

We had our last ride this morning and our first bath
this evening. The baths at Laugarvatn are heated from
the hot springs; with great good sense they do not use the
actual water of the springs (sulphur again!) but with much
ingenuity run some ordinary water through the springs
in pipes. This morning we saw the 250 Frenchmen—the
ones who were coming to breakfast. Many of them were
Germans but even so there were a lot more French than
one expects to see anywhere out of France. They were
mostly middle-aged but included a few miserable girls in
their 'teens whom Greenhalge was able to compare un-
favourably with our ones. They had all motored out the
50 kilometres or so from Reykjavik and had the time of
their lives taking cine-photos of four or five unhappy little
native children togged up in pseudo-national dress and
standing in awkward dumbcrambo attitudes against a blank

wall. The invasion, needless to say, also included a few
middle-aged Englishwomen, the sort with ankles lapping
down over their shoes and a puglike expression of factitious
enthusiasm combined with the determination to be in at
the death, whoever or whatever is dying. Maisie had a
field-day with her Zeiss. And so to Laugarvatn. I had the
little brown pony which I had the first day, and, strange
to say, I now found it extremely comfortable. Greenhalge
fell off twice to-day but the really bad feature of the day
was that the guides produced another cave (they ought
to be psycho-analysed). We entered it by a small burrow
and it took us three-quarters of an hour to reach the other
end of it. It was just as clammy, rugged, incoherent,
dangerous, and dark as the one near Kalmanstunga and
once again we had only one candle. There is nothing to be
said for this type of cave. We saw more caves later however; we went out of our way to see them in fact, branching
up a grassy slope to the left. These ones were rounded
openings in a very soft cinder-coloured stone which I
maintain to be a kind of volcanic sandstone. Maisie says
that a volcanic sandstone is a contradiction in terms; it is
a sad reflection on female education that none of us knows
any geology. One thing we do know however is that you
can't find fossils in Iceland. A pity; a fossil or two would
make the place more homey. Well, till a few years ago
these sandstone or whatever-they-are caves were lived in
by a couple with a cow. The rock is very easy to cut and
you could see where they had cut slots for the door-bars,
also where the cow had spent long nights munching away
the wall. The rock outside, which is of a very odd formation
—quite Barbara Hepworth—is covered with carved
names, names of people and ships and the registration
numbers of cars. Someone has also carefully cut out the
word SILLY and cut a square round it. The road from
here to Laugarvatn was mainly downhill and Maisie and

Anne rode ahead in a spirit of competition; Maisie likes to
show she is not as old as she was. Various signs of civilisation began to appear such as stray agricultural implements. My little pony began to shy; I suppose it thought
they were monsters. I was not at all surprised when we
reached Laugarvatn to hear that Maisie had been thrown
by her horse a hundred yards from home. While galloping
up the straight it suddenly turned at right angles to itself,
leaving Maisie in the air, from which in due time she
descended but, being Maisie, did not break anything or
appear appreciably altered except for a little mud on the
face. The hotel at Laugarvatn is a school in the winter and
an hotel in the summer. It is a very pleasant place but we
are not sleeping in it. The others have put up their own
tents and Maisie and I have hired one of the large tents
which the hotel lets out in the summer to surplus visitors.
This is much more what a tent ought to be. There is a
camp-bed on either side of it plus mattresses plus bolsters,
and there is room to move about in the middle. There are
of course spiders. It is sad to think that they never have
anything but grass and hay to eat. Oh sorry—I must have
left out a sentence. I meant to say that we had said good-
bye to our horses. Not the spiders, you see. Not but what
the spiders must have rather a thin time because there are
very few flies in this country. Perhaps they are Bernard
Shaw spiders. We stood ourselves a dinner in the hotel
instead of making a last inroad on the smoked mutton (by
now rather sordid) and our dried fish who is so tattered he
looks like a scarecrow; he was a fine animal once. Dinner
began with asparagus soup—aren't we getting civilised—
but I was very sorry we had no skyr. Skyr is very good; it
is a near relation of cream cheese and a distant relation of
yaghourt. There were about fifty old women also having
dinner—a kind of mother's union for they were wearing
their national costume which with its gold medallions in

front and long loops of hair behind makes a lady, from my own point of view, look rather too much like a horse. We treated ourselves to some citron and Maisie had an attack of General Knowledge. She told us—what we all knew already—that the population of Iceland is 110,000 of which 30,000 live in Reykjavik. Mary wanted to know how they knew this. I am getting just a *teeny* bit tired of communing with the budding mind of youth. The conversation of the young has no doubt a certain artless charm which pleases for the length of a tea-party but when prolonged all the way round the Langjökull it suffers from the two minor flaws of being (*a*) invariably platitudinous and (*b*) infinitely repetitive. They are all getting terribly excited about their train-connections at Hull; to-morrow, you see, they are sailing for home. I think they are banking too much on their boat running to schedule. No doubt as far as *place* goes it will be reasonably accurate and land them in Hull and not in Fishguard but I should allow a good 36 hours' margin for time. They are only *little* boats after all. I can hear the young now; they are lying in their tents next door, writing up their diaries. Two of them are talking about Miss Robinson. Anne is going to stay behind to-morrow. She and Maisie and I have an invitation to stay in the lunatic asylum. I shall send this letter with Miss Greenhalge on the *Godafoss*. Good-night, liebchen.

August 27th

    'And so the game is ended that should not have begun.' We are now on the *Godafoss* seeing off our party. You will notice that the boat is leaving a day late; it probably stopped round the coast to pick up some fish-heads (Icelandic boats have the courage of their caprices). I am writing this with a blunt pencil leaning against the taff-rail (?). Yesterday morning we bussed back from Laugarvatn to Reykjavik and heard the sad news about the boat.

Greenhalge and the girls spent the night in the students' hostel, Maisie and Anne and I accepted our invitation to the asylum, where Maisie fell through her bed; it was a camp-bed and no doubt took against Maisie for being a pacifist. The Lunatic Asylum is charmingly situated at Kleppur and is quite fittingly the place where Marshal Balbo landed on his flight across the Atlantic. The Reykjavik-Kleppur bus is designed like a cathedral; there are a few seats scattered here and there down the side-aisles and a vast empty space down the middle for people to stand in. The road to Kleppur suffers from ribbon development and nothing, my dear, can look worse than a corrugated iron suburb if it is not kept tidy. The lunatics here are not much in evidence though they can be heard faintly cooing in the distance. They have a very fine bathroom. Our host, the doctor in charge, is a charming old man and so are all his family. He has whitish-grey hair, gold-rimmed spectacles, fiery blue eyes, a bad leg, and a black velvet smoking-jacket. M. thinks he looks rather like W. B. Yeats. That perhaps is because he also is said to be clairvoyant. Spiritualism, you know, has a great vogue in Iceland though they only have their séances in the winter—like the hunting season in England. There is a famous mystic called Dr. Helgi Pjeturrs who has written a book about life on the other planets. Icelanders, he says, are the most spiritual people in the world, but, spiritual or not, we all go to the planets when we die and there we all have a very good time. Dr. Sveinsson however (our asylum doctor) did not talk to us much about spiritualism but indulged his other passion, which is Latin. He has a habit of breaking into Latin in conversation which is a little embarrassing for Maisie and me whose classics are distinctly what you might call rusty. As for that poor girl Anne, she merely goes red in the face and says, 'I'm awfully sorry, I'm afraid I'm jolly bad at it.' It is very impressive

196

however the way Dr. S. will suddenly turn to you over his coffee and remark with terrific gusto, 'Juppiter iratus buccas inflat' or 'Multae sunt viae ingeni humani.' His pronunciation, I may remark, is Icelandic. He showed us his English-Latin grammar, a mid-nineteenth century book by one Roby, which he says is a poem to him. When Dr. S. was a young man he used to act as a guide and take visitors round the country on ponies. He had some very good stories about an old English eccentric he was guide to every summer—a hot-tempered gentleman who used to hit people with hunting-whips but he was so short-sighted he always hit the wrong ones. Mrs. S. was very charming and hospitable and we had bilberries and cream and coffee before going to bed. Then came Maisie's episode with the bed. This morning we came in to Reykjavik and spent the whole morning drinking coffee in the Tea-Rooms, which is their actual name, and eating cream-cakes. We hear that last night two men in Reykjavik got drunk, one betted the other he would swim 100 metres in the harbour, jumped in, swam 50 and was drowned. . . . I must finish this off as the boat has begun to groan. (I don't blame it.) The girls are being seen off by a schoolmate who dropped on them out of the blue in Reykjavik and apparently is staying with friends here—a boring little girl who poses as rather fast and has begun using lipstick, needless to say very badly. Well, darling, goodbye—I don't suppose you will ever read all this stuff—give my love to Cicely. I hope to see you anon in Cambridge or Gordon Square, all my love till then,

HETTY

Chapter XIII

Letter to Lord Byron

PART IV

A ship again; this time the *Dettifoss*.
    Grierson can buy it; all the sea I mean,
All this Atlantic that we've now to cross
    Heading for England's pleasant pastures green.
    Pro tem I've done with the Icelandic scene;
I watch the hills receding in the distance,
I hear the thudding of an engine's pistons.

I hope I'm better, wiser for the trip:
    I've had the benefit of northern breezes,
The open road and good companionship,
    I've seen some very pretty little pieces;
    And though the luck was almost all MacNeice's,
I've spent some jolly evenings playing rummy—
No one can talk at Bridge, unless it's Dummy.

I've learnt to ride, at least to ride a pony,
    Taken a lot of healthy exercise,
On barren mountains and in valleys stony,
    I've tasted a hot spring (a taste was wise),
    And foods a man remembers till he dies.
All things considered, I consider Iceland,
Apart from Reykjavik, a very nice land.

The part can stand as symbol for the whole:
    So ruminating in these last few weeks,
I see the map of all my youth unroll,
    The mental mountains and the psychic creeks,
    The towns of which the master never speaks,
The various parishes and what they voted for,
The colonies, their size, and what they're noted for.

A child may ask when our strange epoch passes,
    During a history lesson, 'Please, sir, what's
An intellectual of the middle classes?
    Is he a maker of ceramic pots
    Or does he choose his king by drawing lots?'
What follows now may set him on the rail,
A plain, perhaps a cautionary, tale.

My passport says I'm five feet and eleven,
    With hazel eyes and fair (it's tow-like) hair,
That I was born in York in 1907,
    With no distinctive markings anywhere.
    Which isn't quite correct. Conspicuous there
On my right cheek appears a large brown mole,
I think I don't dislike it on the whole.

My father's forbears were all Midland yeomen
    Till royalties from coal mines did them good;
I think they must have been phlegmatic slowmen.
    My mother's ancestors had Norman blood,
    From Somerset I've always understood;
My grandfathers on either side agree
In being clergymen and C. of E.

Father and Mother each was one of seven,
    Though one died young and one was not all there;
Their fathers both went suddenly to Heaven

While they were still quite small and left them here
    To work on earth with little cash to spare;
A nurse, a rising medico, at Bart's
Both felt the pangs of Cupid's naughty darts.

My home then was professional and 'high'.
    No gentler father ever lived, I'll lay
All Lombard Street against a shepherd's pie.
    We imitate our loves: well, neighbours say
    I grow more like my mother every day.
I don't like business men. I know a Prot
Will never really kneel, but only squat.

In pleasures of the mind they both delighted;
    The library in the study was enough
To make a better boy than me short-sighted;
    Our old cook Ada surely knew her stuff;
    My elder brothers did not treat me rough;
We lived at Solihull, a village then;
Those at the gasworks were my favourite men.

My earliest recollection to stay put
    Is of a white stone doorstep and a spot
Of pus where father lanced the terrier's foot;
    Next, stuffing shag into the coffee pot.
    Which nearly killed my mother, but did not;
Both psycho-analyst and Christian minister,
Will think these incidents extremely sinister.

With northern myths my little brain was laden,
    With deeds of Thor and Loki and such scenes;
My favourite tale was Andersen's *Ice Maiden*;
    But better far than any kings or queens
    I liked to see and know about machines:
And from my sixth until my sixteenth year
I thought myself a mining engineer.

The mine I always pictured was for lead,
    Though copper mines might, faute de mieux, be sound.
To-day I like a weight upon my bed;
    I always travel by the Underground;
    For concentration I have always found
A small room best, the curtains drawn, the light on;
Then I can work from nine till tea-time, right on.

I must admit that I was most precocious
    (Precocious children rarely grow up good).
My aunts and uncles thought me quite atrocious
    For using words more adult than I should;
    My first remark at school did all it could
To shake a matron's monumental poise;
'I like to see the various types of boys.'

The Great War had begun: but masters' scrutiny
    And fists of big boys were the war to us;
It was as harmless as the Indian Mutiny,
    A beating from the Head was dangerous.
    But once when half the form put down *Bellus*.
We were accused of that most deadly sin,
Wanting the Kaiser and the Huns to win.

The way in which we really were affected
    Was having such a varied lot to teach us.
The best were fighting, as the King expected,
    The remnant either elderly grey creatures,
    Or characters with most peculiar features.
Many were raggable, a few were waxy,
One had to leave abruptly in a taxi.

Surnames I must not write—O Reginald,
    You at least taught us that which fadeth not,
Our earliest visions of the great wide world;

The beer and biscuits that your favourites got,
    Your tales revealing you a first-class shot,
Your riding breeks, your drama called *The Waves*,
A few of us will carry to our graves.

'Half a lunatic, half a knave'. No doubt
    A holy terror to the staff at tea;
A good headmaster must have soon found out
    Your moral character was all at sea;
    I question if you'd got a pass degree:
But little children bless your kind that knocks
Away the edifying stumbling blocks.

How can I thank you? For it only shows
    (Let me ride just this once my hobby-horse),
There're things a good headmaster never knows.
    There must be sober schoolmasters, of course,
    But what a prep school really puts across
Is knowledge of the world we'll soon be lost in:
To-day it's more like Dickens than Jane Austen.

I hate the modern trick, to tell the truth,
    Of straightening out the kinks in the young mind,
Our passion for the tender plant of youth,
    Our hatred for all weeds of any kind.
    Slogans are bad: the best that I can find
Is this: 'Let each child have that's in our care
As much neurosis as the child can bear.'

In this respect, at least, my bad old Adam is
    Pigheadedly against the general trend;
And has no use for all these new academies
    Where readers of the better weeklies send
    The child they probably did not intend,
To paint a lampshade, marry, or keep pigeons,
Or make a study of the world religions.

Goddess of bossy underlings, Normality!
    What murders are committed in thy name!
Totalitarian is thy state Reality,
    Reeking of antiseptics and the shame
    Of faces that all look and feel the same.
Thy Muse is one unknown to classic histories,
The topping figure of the hockey mistress.

From thy dread Empire not a soul's exempted:
    More than the nursemaids pushing prams in parks,
By thee the intellectuals are tempted,
    O, to commit the treason of the clerks,
    Bewitched by thee to literary sharks.
But I must leave thee to thy office stool,
I must get on now to my public school.

Men had stopped throwing stones at one another,
    Butter and Father had come back again;
Gone were the holidays we spent with Mother
    In furnished rooms on mountain, moor, and fen;
    And gone those summer Sunday evenings, when
Along the seafronts fled a curious noise,
'Eternal Father', sung by three young boys.

Nation spoke Peace, or said she did, with nation;
    The sexes tried their best to look the same;
Morals lost value during the inflation,
    The great Victorians kindly took the blame;
    Visions of Dada to the Post-War came,
Sitting in cafés, nostrils stuffed with bread,
Above the recent and the straight-laced dead.

I've said my say on public schools elsewhere:
    Romantic friendship, prefects, bullying,
I shall not deal with, c'est une autre affaire.
    Those who expect them, will get no such thing,

It is the strictly relevant I sing.
Why should they grumble? They've the Greek Anthology,
And all the spicier bits of Anthropology.

We all grow up the same way, more or less;
    Life is not known to give away her presents;
She only swops. The unself-consciousness
    That children share with animals and peasants
    Sinks in the 'stürm und drang' of Adolescence.
Like other boys I lost my taste for sweets,
Discovered sunsets, passion, God, and Keats.

I shall recall a single incident
    No more. I spoke of mining engineering
As the career on which my mind was bent,
    But for some time my fancies had been veering;
    Mirages of the future kept appearing;
Crazes had come and gone in short, sharp gales,
For motor-bikes, photography, and whales.

But indecision broke off with a clean-cut end
    One afternoon in March at half-past three
When walking in a ploughed field with a friend;
    Kicking a little stone, he turned to me
    And said, 'Tell me, do you write poetry?'
I never had, and said so, but I knew
That very moment what I wished to do.

Without a bridge passage this leads me straight
    Into the theme marked 'Oxford' on my score
From pages twenty-five to twenty-eight.
    Aesthetic trills I'd never heard before
    Rose from the strings, shrill poses from the cor;
The woodwind chattered like a pre-war Russian,
'Art' boomed the brass, and 'Life' thumped the percussion.

204

A raw provincial, my good taste was tardy,
    And Edward Thomas I as yet preferred;
I was still listening to Thomas Hardy
    Putting divinity about a bird;
    But Eliot spoke the still unspoken word;
For gasworks and dried tubers I forsook
The clock at Grantchester, the English rook.

All youth's intolerant certainty was mine as
    I faced life in a double-breasted suit;
I bought and praised but did not read Aquinas,
    At the *Criterion's* verdict I was mute,
    Though Arnold's I was ready to refute;
And through the quads dogmatic words rang clear,
'Good poetry is classic and austere.'

So much for Art. Of course Life had its passions too;
    The student's flesh like his imagination
Makes facts fit theories and has fashions too.
    We were the tail, a sort of poor relation
    To that debauched, eccentric generation
That grew up with their fathers at the War,
And made new glosses on the noun Amor.

Three years passed quickly while the Isis went
    Down to the sea for better or for worse;
Then to Berlin, not Carthage, I was sent
    With money from my parents in my purse,
    And ceased to see the world in terms of verse.
I met a chap called Layard and he fed
New doctrines into my receptive head.

Part came from Lane, and part from D. H. Lawrence;
    Gide, though I didn't know it then, gave part.
They taught me to express my deep abhorrence
    If I caught anyone preferring Art
    To Life and Love and being Pure-in-Heart.

I lived with crooks but seldom was molested;
The Pure-in-Heart can never be arrested.

He's gay; no bludgeonings of chance can spoil it,
    The Pure-in-Heart loves all men on a par,
And has no trouble with his private toilet;
    The Pure-in-Heart is never ill; catarrh
    Would be the yellow streak, the brush of tar;
Determined to be loving and forgiving,
I came back home to try and earn my living.

The only thing you never turned your hand to
    Was teaching English in a boarding school.
To-day it's a profession that seems grand to
    Those whose alternative's an office stool;
    For budding authors it's become the rule.
To many an unknown genius postmen bring
Typed notices from Rabbitarse and String.

The Head's M.A., a bishop is a patron,
    The assistant staff is highly qualified;
Health is the care of an experienced matron,
    The arts are taught by ladies from outside;
    The food is wholesome and the grounds are wide;
The aim is training character and poise,
With special coaching for the backward boys.

I found the pay good and had time to spend it,
    Though others may not have the good luck I did:
For you I'd hesitate to recommend it;
    Several have told me that they can't abide it.
    Still, if one tends to get a bit one-sided,
It's pleasant as it's easy to secure
The hero worship of the immature.

More, it's a job, and jobs to-day are rare:
    All the ideals in the world won't feed us

Although they give our crimes a certain air.
    So barons of the press who know their readers
    Employ to write their more appalling leaders,
Instead of Satan's horned and hideous minions,
Clever young men of liberal opinions.

Which brings me up to nineteen-thirty-five;
    Six months of film work is another story
I can't tell now. But, here I am, alive
    Knowing the true source of that sense of glory
    That still surrounds the England of the Tory,
Come only to the rather tame conclusion
That no man by himself has life's solution.

I know—the fact is really not unnerving—
    That what is done is done, that no past dies,
That what we see depends on who's observing,
    And what we think on our activities.
    That envy warps the virgin as she dries
But 'Post coitum, homo tristis' means
The lover must go carefully with the greens.

The boat has brought me to the landing-stage,
    Up the long estuary of mud and sedges;
The line I travel has the English gauge;
    The engine's shadow vaults the little hedges;
    And summer's done. I sign the usual pledges
To be a better poet, better man;
I'll really do it this time if I can.

I hope this reaches you in your abode,
    This letter that's already far too long,
Just like the Prelude or the Great North Road;
    But here I end my conversational song.
    I hope you don't think mail from strangers wrong.
As to its length, I tell myself you'll need it,
You've all eternity in which to read it.

END OF PART IV

Chapter XIV

Letter to Kristjan Andresson, Esq.

—————◆◆◆—————

My Dear Kristjan Andresson,

In Reykjavik I made you a promise that I would send you my impressions of your country, and now I am back at home I must do my best to fulfil it, a small return indeed for all your unwearied hospitality to us, and for your wife's delicious pancakes. Though I question whether the reactions of the tourist are of much value; without employment in the country he visits, his knowledge of its economic and social relations is confined to the study of official statistics and the gossip of tea-tables; ignorant of the language his judgment of character and culture is limited to the superficial; and the length of his visit, in my case only three months, precludes him from any real intimacy with his material. At the best he only observes what the inhabitants know already; at the worst he is guilty of glib generalisations based on inadequate and often incorrect data. Moreover, whatever his position in his own country, the social status of a tourist in a foreign land is always that of a rentier—as far as his hosts are concerned he is a person of independent means—and he will see them with a rentier's eye: the price of a meal or the civility of a porter will strike him more forcibly than a rise in the number of cancer cases or the corruption of the judicial machine. Finally the remoteness of Iceland, coupled with its literary and political history, make it a country which, if visited at all, is visited by people with strong, and usually romantic, preconceptions. Few English people take an interest in Iceland, but in those few the interest is passionate. My father, for example, is such a one, and some of the most vivid recollections of my childhood are hearing him read to me Icelandic folk-tales and sagas, and I know more about Northern mythology than Greek. Archbishop van Kroil, who visited Iceland in 1772, makes an observation which all tourists would do well to remember—

'You must not', he says, 'in this place apply to me the story which Helvetius tells of a clergyman and a fine lady who together observed the spots in the moon, which the former took for church steeples and the latter for a pair of happy lovers. I know that we frequently imagine to have really found what we most think of, or most wish for.' He might have further added, that when we fail to find it we often rush to the opposite extreme of disappointment.

I do not intend to expatiate upon the natural beauties of your island: to you they need no advertisement and for the tourist there are many guide books; the Great Geysir will draw its crowds without any help from me. Besides, there is an English poem with the sentiments of which I entirely sympathise.

> Biography
> Is better than Geography,
> Geography's about maps,
> Biography's about chaps.

As I am going to be frank about what I disliked, I must say at once that I enjoyed my visit enormously; that, except on one minor occasion, I met with unvarying kindness and hospitality; and that as far as the people themselves are concerned, I can think of none among whom I should prefer to be exiled.

Physique and Clothes

I find the physical standard of the Icelanders, both in health and looks, high compared with most European countries, but not as high perhaps as the Norwegians. On the whole the men seem better looking than the women. It is all the more pity, therefore, that the average taste in clothes should be so poor. I know that Englishwomen are the worst dressed in the world, but that is no excuse for Iceland. I have seldom seen worse clothes, for both sexes, than I saw in the shops in Reykjavik; flashier and more discordant in colour. This is, I know partly a question of money, but not entirely. The Icelandic women could be twice as well dressed for the same expenditure.

Character

This is a silly thing to write about. I can't believe that the character of one nation is much different from that of another, or does not have the same variations. In any case the tourist sees nothing important. Like others before me I admired nearly all the farmers I met enormously; I saw none of that boorishness and yokel stupidity that one sees in the country in England. On the other hand I felt that many of the people in the towns were demoralised by living in them. This is natural. Towns take a lot of getting used to, and one must be much richer, if one is to live decently in them, than one need be in the country. The two obvious faults I noticed were unpunctuality, which is trivial, and drunkenness, which is silly but not to be wondered at when it is almost impossible to get a decent drink in the country. The beer is filthy, wine is prohibitive in price, and there is nothing left but whisky, which is not a good drink.

Letter to Kristian Andreirsson, Esq.

A Norwegian fish merchant told me that he did not like doing business with Icelanders, but personally I found them more honest than most people I have met. I am told that politics are very corrupt—natural perhaps in a country where everyone knows everyone else personally—but I have no means of verifying or contradicting this.

As regards their emotional life, I found the Icelander, certainly as compared with the Englishman, very direct, normal, and free from complexes, but whether that is a good or a bad thing, I cannot decide.

Manners

The Icelander seems to me to have beautiful natural manners, but rather imperfect artificial ones. By artificial ones, I mean those which do not depend on an instinctive feeling for other people, but have to be learnt for a complicated social life. Mackenzie, writing in 1810, said: 'The unrestrained evacuation of saliva seems to be a fashion all over Iceland.' It seems to be so still.

Wealth and Class Distinctions

It is an observation frequently made by bourgeois visitors that in Iceland there are no rich and no poor. At first sight this seems to be true. There are no mansions like those in Mayfair, and no hovels like those in the East End. Wages and the general standard of living are high in comparison with other countries; and there is less apparent class distinction than in any other capitalist country. But when one remembers that Iceland has an area larger than Ireland, a population smaller than Brighton, and some of the richest fishing grounds in the world, one is not convinced that the wages could not be higher and the differences less. I saw plenty of people whose standard of living I should not like to have to share, and a few whose wealth made them arrogant, ostentatious, and vulgar. In

Letter to Kristian Andreirsson, Esq.

England there are certain traditional ways of living and spending for rich people which at least give them a certain grace. In Iceland there are none.

Education and Culture

The home of some of the finest prose in the world, with a widespread knowledge of verse and its technique, and 100% literacy, Iceland has every reason to be proud of herself, and if I make certain criticisms, it is not because I do not appreciate their achievements, but because from a country which has done so much one expects still more. In education my general impression was that the general standard was high; and I think the custom of students working on farms in the summer should provide the best possible balance of academic and manual education—indeed under these unusual circumstances I should like to see the academic education more classical—Greek and manual labour seem to me the best kind of education. But the higher grades, the sixth form and University teaching do not seem to me so good. I know this is almost entirely a question of money. The only suggestion I can make is that there should be a special school for bright children, picked from all over the island by a scholarship examination.

As regards general culture, it is high, but not as high as some accounts would lead one to believe. While in the country I heard a kitchen-maid give an excellent criticism of a medieval saga, in the towns on the other hand, particularly Reykjavik, there were obviously many people who had lost their specifically Icelandic culture, and had gained no other. In general, while literature seems fairly widely appreciated, there is almost no architecture, no drama, and little knowledge of painting or music.

I know that this is inevitable. I know that the day of a self-contained national culture is over, that Iceland is far from Europe, that the first influences of Europe are always the worst ones, and that the development of a truly European culture is slow and expensive. But I am convinced that the cultural future of Iceland depends on the extent to which she can absorb the best of the European traditions, and make them her own.

The only suggestions I can make have probably been thought of before, but I give them for what they may be worth.

Owing to currency problems, it is difficult for Icelanders to buy books. Apart from the local town libraries, therefore, there should be one first-class lending library of the best European books, particularly contemporary, serving the whole of the island.

Obviously Iceland cannot afford to buy pictures, but to-day reproductions are so good that they could with great profit be placed in galleries and schools. Music is more difficult. The Broadcasting Station does much with gramophone records, but could I think do more. I don't like the Scandinavian passion for male choirs, which cuts one off from the vast bulk of choral music.

Lastly, a small country like Iceland should be an ideal place for a really live drama—as in Ireland. This depends solely on writers—of whom there are plenty—and a few enthusiastic amateurs in a small room. To start by building an enormous state theatre which you can't afford to finish, is starting at the wrong end.

General

Most of the books about Iceland which I have read speak as if it were a nation of farmers. In point of fact, the majority live in towns, and pretty grim a town like Siglufjordur is too. To me this is the most important fact about Iceland. The present time is a critical one. I see what was once a society and a culture of independent peasant proprietors, becoming, inevitably, urbanised and in danger of becoming—not so inevitably—proletaria- nised for the benefit of a few, who on account of their small number and geographical isolation, can never build up a capitalist culture of their own.

A town and a town life which are worth having are expensive, and in a small and not conspicuously wealthy country like Iceland I am inclined to believe that they can only be realised by anyone, let alone the masses, in a socialist community.

Well, then, here are my impressions. I have tried to express them as simply and directly as I could, and can only hope that you will be less conscious of their super- ficiality than I am.

When next you come to England I shall have my revenge by making you do the same for me.

With kindest regards to your wife and yourself,

Yours sincerely,

W. H. A.

Chapter XV

Letter to William Coldstream, Esq.

————◆◆◆◆————

Now the three ride from Hraensnef to Reykholt where they stayed two nights. Thence they went to Reykjavik and took ship to Isafjordur. Joachim was the vice-consul, a man well spoken of. He found them a motor-boat to take them to Melgraseyri in Isafjördardjup. The name of the farmer was Olafur. He had six foster children. Louis fell sick and remained in his bed but Auden and Michael rode to Ormuli where they were very hospitably entertained. After three days they all returned to Isafjördur and dwelt at the Salvation Army Hostel there. They did not go out of doors much but spent the day drinking brandy and playing cards. People said they had not behaved very well. Now it is the end of summer and they sail oversea to England. In the summer Louis and Auden published a book.

This, Bill, is a little donnish experiment in objective narrative.

'But Landscape,' cries the Literary Supplement,
                'You must have Landscape':
And the historian of the Human Consciousness;
'You can't put the clock back. Not since Montaigne';
And the reviewer taking the Russians out of a hamper;
                'It's simply not Tolstoi':

And the professional novelist in a flash;
     'Too easy. No dialogue.'
And the common reader yawning;
     'I want more love life.'

But Landscape's so dull
   if you haven't Lawrence's wonderful wooziness.
My private reflections are only what you'd expect from an
  artist and a gentleman.
The poet's eye is not one from which nothing is hid
Nor the straightforward diary of a nice English schoolboy
  really much use.
And love life—I'm sorry, dear reader—is something
    I always soft pedal.

But Horrebow came here and wrote a chapter on snakes
    The chapter has only one sentence.
Hooker came here and made a list of the plants
Henderson came here with Bibles
And looked at the Geysir and thought
     'The Lord could stop that if he wanted'
Lord Dufferin got tight with the Governor and spoke in
    dog-latin
And Morris opened his letters from England
    And wondered at people's calmness.
They can get them all from a public library
This letter's for you.

A reminder of Soho Square and that winter in horrible
  London
When we sat in the back passage pretending to work
While the camera boys told dirty stories
And George capped them all with his one of the major in
  India
Who went to a ball with dysentery
    told it in action

217

Till we sneaked out for coffee and discussed our colleagues
And were suspected, quite rightly, of being disloyal.
Especially you, whose tongue is the most malicious I know.

But after we'd torn them to pieces, we turned our atten-
tion to Art
Upstairs in the Corner House, in the hall with the phallic
pillars
And before the band had finished a pot pourri from
Wagner
We'd scrapped Significant Form, and voted for Subject,
Hence really this letter.

I'm bringing a problem.
Call it as Henry James might have done in a preface
The Presentation of the Given Subject
The problem of every writer of travels;
For Life and his publisher hand him his theme on a plate:
'You went to such and such places with so-and-so
And such and such things occurred.
Now do what you can.'
But I can't.

The substantial facts are as I have stated above
No bandits, no comic passport officials
No hairbreadth escapes, the only test of endurance
A sixteen mile scramble in gumboots to look at dead
whales
No monuments and only a little literary history
Gisli the Soursop was killed on the other side of the moun-
tains
No views? O dozens of course. But I sympathise with the
sailors
  '*Instead of a girl or two in a taxi*
  We were compelled to look at the Black Sea, and the
  Black Sea
  Isn't all it's cracked up to be.'

Letter to William Coldstream, Esq.

An artist you said, if I remember you rightly,
An artist you said, in the waiting room at Euston
Looking towards that dictator's dream of a staircase
An artist you said, is both perceiver and teller, the spy and
    the gossip
Something between the slavey in Daumier's caricature
                The one called *Nadadada*
And the wife of a minor canon.

Very well then, let's start with perceiving
Let me pretend that I'm the impersonal eye of the camera
Sent out by God to shoot on location
And we'll look at the rushes together.

Face of an Icelandic Professor
Like a child's self expression in plasticine
              A child from the bottom form.
Then a lot out of focus.
Now a pan round a typical sitting-room
Bowl of postcards on table—Harmonium with Brahm's
    Sapphic Ode
Pi-picture—little girl crosses broken ravine bridge pro-
    tected by angel.
Cut to saddling ponies—close up of farmer's hands at a
    girth strap
Dissolve to long shot of Reykholt school
              Corbusier goes all Northern.
Close up of Gynaecologist Angler offering me brandy
In the next war he said
There'd be one anaesthetist to at least four tables.
Mid-shot of fox farm
      Black foxes in coops—white tips to their tails
The rest N. G. I'm afraid.
Now there is a whaling station during the lunch hour
      The saw is for cutting up jaw-bones

The whole place was slippery with filth—with guts and
    decaying flesh—
                like an artist's palette—
We were tired as you see and in shocking tempers.
Patreksfjördur by moonlight, shot as the boat left.
Night effects, though I say it, pretty O.K.
Our favourite occupation—the North Pole Café
I've got some shots later of hands of rummy—
        Louis's scandalous luck caused a lot of ill feeling.
Now going up Isafjördardjup—the motorboat cost 40
    kronur.
The hills are a curious shape—like vaulting-horses in a
    gymnasium
                The light was rotten.
What on earth is all this? O yes, a dog fight at one of the
    farms
Too confused to show much.
O and this is Louis drawing the Joker as usual.
And here's a shot for the Chief—epic, the *Drifters* tradition
The end of a visit, the motor-boat's out of the screen on the
    left
It was blowing a hurricane.
Harbour at Isafjördur—late summer evening
'Tatty', Basil would call it I think, but I rather like it.

Well. That's the lot.
As you see, no crisis, no continuity.
Only heroic cutting could save it
Perhaps MacNaughten might do it
            Or Legge.
But I've cut a few stills out, in case they'd amuse you.

So much for perceiving. Now telling. That's easy.

Louis read George Eliot in bed
And Michael and I climbed the cliff behind Hraensnef

And *I was* so frightened, my dear.

And we all rowed on the lake and giggled because the boat
    leaked

And the farmer was angry when we whipped his horses

And Louis had a dream—unrepeatable but he repeated it—

And the lady at table had diabetes, poor thing

And Louis dreamt of a bedroom with four glass walls

And I was upset because they told me I didn't look
    innocent

(I liked it really of course)

And the whaling station wouldn't offer us any coffee

And Michael didn't speak for three hours after that

And the first motor-boat we hired turned back because of
    the weather

'A hot spot' he said but we and the vice consul didn't
    believe him

And that cost an extra ten kronur.

And it was after ten when we really got there and could
    discover a landing

And we walked up to the farm in the dark

Over a new mown meadow, the dogs running in and out of
    the lamplight

And I woke in the night to hear Louis vomiting
                  Something like a ship siren

And I played 'O Isis and Osiris' on the harmonium next
    day

And we read the short stories of Somerset Maugham
    aloud to each other

And the best one was called *His Excellency*.

And I said to Michael 'All power corrupts' and he was very
    angry about it.

And he ate thirty-two cakes in an afternoon

And the soup they gave us the last day tasted of hair oil

And we had to wrap the salt fish in an envelope not to hurt
    their feelings

And we stayed at the Salvation Army—notices: no cards
   allowed,
                  So we played in our bedroom
And we drank Spanish brandy out of our tooth mugs,
   trying to like it
And feeling like schoolboys, hiding our sins from the maid.
And the film that night was in English, and the lovers
   were very vehement
But the loud speaker was badly adjusted and they
   squawked like hens
And Louis stood on the quay muttering Greek in his beard
Like a character out of the Cantos—
ἀλλὰ καὶ ὡς ἐθέλω καὶ ἐέλδομαι ἤματα πάντα
οἴκαδε τ' ἐλθέμεναι καὶ ἰδεσθαι νόστιμον ἦμαρ.

But that wasn't the only thing he said
Back at Hraensnef after a heavy silence
He suddenly spoke. 'God made the mice,' he said
'And the mice made the Scheiss'
And again he said 'The dark lady of the Bonnets'
And Michael said 'You like nothing
But smoking, drinking coffee, and writing'
And he wrote on my postcard to Christopher 'We have our
   moods.'

That's all except the orchestral background
The news from Europe interwoven with our behaving
The pleasant voice of the wireless announcer, like a con-
   sultant surgeon
      'Your case is hopeless. I give you six months.'
And the statements of famous economists;
Like cook coming in and saying triumphantly
      'Rover's taken the joint, ma'am.'
That's all the externals, and they're not my pigeon
While the purely subjective feelings,
The heart-felt exultations and the short despairs

Require a musician. Bach, say, or Schubert.
But here is my poem, nevertheless, the fruit of that fort-
    night
And one too of Louis's, for comparative reading.
The novelist has one way of stating experience,
The film director another
These are our versions—each man to his medium.

    'O who can ever gaze his fill',
        Farmer and fisherman say,
    'On native shore and local hill,
    Grudge aching limb or callus on the hand?
    Fathers, grandfathers stood upon this land,
    And here the pilgrims from our loins shall stand.'
        So farmer and fisherman say
        In their fortunate heyday:
        But Death's soft answer drifts across
        Empty catch or harvest loss
          Or an unlucky May.

*   The earth is an oyster with nothing inside it*
*   Not to be born is the best for man*
*   The end of toil is a bailiff's order*
*   Throw down the mattock and dance while you can.*

    'O life's too short for friends who share',
        Travellers think in their hearts,
    'The city's common bed, the air,
    The mountain bivouac and the bathing beach,
    Where incidents draw every day from each
    Memorable gesture and witty speech.'
        So travellers think in their hearts,
        Till malice or circumstance parts
        Them from their constant humour:
        And shyly Death's coercive rumour
          In the silence starts.

A friend is the old old tale of Narcissus
  Not to be born is the best for man
An active partner in something disgraceful
  Change your partner, dance while you can.

'O stretch your hands across the sea,'
    The impassioned lover cries,
'Stretch them towards your harm and me.
Our grass is green, and sensual our brief bed,
The stream sings at its foot, and at its head
The mild and vegetarian beasts are fed.'
    So the impassioned lover cries
    Till his storm of pleasure dies:
    From the bedpost and the rocks
    Death's enticing echo mocks,
        And his voice replies.

The greater the love, the more false to its object
  Not to be born is the best for man
After the kiss comes the impulse to throttle
  Break the embraces, dance while you can.

'I see the guilty world forgiven,'
    Dreamer and drunkard sing,
'The ladders let down out of heaven;
The laurel springing from the martyrs' blood;
The children skipping where the weepers stood;
The lovers natural, and the beasts all good.'
    So dreamer and drunkard sing
    Till day their sobriety bring:
    Parrotwise with death's reply
    From whelping fear and nesting lie,
        Woods and their echoes ring.

The desires of the heart are as crooked as corkscrews
  Not to be born is the best for man

The second best is a formal order
  The dance's pattern, dance while you can.
Dance, dance, for the figure is easy
  The tune is catching and will not stop
Dance till the stars come down with the rafters
  Dance, dance, dance till you drop.

W. H. A.

Iceland

No shields now
  Cross the knoll,
The hills are dull
  With leaden shale,
Whose arms could squeeze
  The breath from time
And the climb is long
  From cairn to cairn.

Houses are few
  But decorous
In a ruined land
  Of sphagnum moss;
Corrugated iron
  Farms inherit
The spirit and phrase
  Of ancient sagas

Men have forgotten
  Anger and ambush,
To make ends meet
  Their only business:
The lover riding
  In the lonely dale
Hears the plover's
  Single pipe

And feels perhaps
But undefined
The drift of death
In the sombre wind
Deflating the trim
Balloon of lust
In a grey storm
Of dust and grit.

So we who have come
As trippers North
Have minds no match
For this land's girth;
The glacier's licking
Tongues deride
Our pride of life,
Our flashy songs.

But the people themselves
Who live here
Ignore the brooding
Fear, the sphinx;
And the radio
With tags of tune
Defies their pillared
Basalt crags.

Whose ancestors
Thought that at last
The end would come
To a blast of horns
And gods would face
The worst in fight,
Vanish in the night
The last, the first

Night which began
  Without device
In ice and rocks,
  No shade or shape;
Grass and blood,
  The strife of life,
Were an interlude
  Which soon must pass

And all go back
  Relapse to rock
Under the shawl
  Of the ice-caps,
The cape which night
  Will spread to cover
The world when the living
  Flags are furled.

L. M.

Chapter XVI

Auden and MacNeice: Their Last Will and Testament

◆◆◆◆

We, Wystan Hugh Auden and Louis MacNeice,
Brought up to speak and write the English tongue
Being led in the eighteenth year of the Western
    Peace

To the duck-shaped mountainous island with the
    Danish King,
At Melgraseyri in Isafjördardjup
Under the eaves of a glacier, considering

The autumns, personal and public, which already
    creep
Through city-crowded Europe, and those in want
Who soon must look up at the winter sky and weep,

Do set down this, our will and testament:
Believing man responsible for what he does,
Sole author of his terror and his content.

The duty his to learn, to make his choice;
On each the guilt of failure, and in each the power
To shape, create and move, love and rejoice.

Poor prospects now have any who would insure
Against the blight of crops—blood in the furrows—
And who knows which of our legacies will endure?

First to our ancestors who lie in barrows
Or under nameless cairns on heathery hills
Or where the seal-swim crashes the island-narrows

Or in Jacobean tomb, whose scrolls and skulls
Carry off death with an elegant inscription,
The Latin phrasing which beguiles and dulls

The bitter regrets at the loved body's corruption
Or those who merely share the prayer that is
        muttered
For many sunk together in war's eruption,

To all, clay-bound or chalk-bound, stiff or scattered,
We leave the values of their periods,
The things which seemed to them the things that
        mattered,

Pride in family and in substantial goods,
Comfort, ambition, honour and elegance,
The jealous eye upon wives and private woods,

The hand alert for vengeance, the brow which once
Contracted was unforgiving, proud of extremes
Not bearing easily the deserter or the dunce.

L.   And to my own in particular whose rooms
Were whitewashed, small, soothed with the smoke of
        peat,
Looking out on the Atlantic's gleams and glooms,

Of whom some lie among brambles high remote
Above the yellow falls of Ballysodare
Whose hands were hard with handling cart and boat

I leave the credit for that which may endure
Within myself of peasant vitality and
Of the peasant's sense of humour and I am sure

That those forefathers clamped in the boggy ground
Should have my thanks for any Ariadne's thread
Of instinct following which I too have found

My way through the forking paths of briars and mud,
My thanks I leave them therefore double and next
I leave my father half my pride of blood

And also my admiration who has fixed
His pulpit out of the reach of party slogans
And all the sordid challenges and the mixed

Motives of those who bring their drums and dragons
To silence moderation and free speech
Bawling from armoured cars and carnival wagons;

And to my stepmother I leave her rich
Placid delight in detailed living who adds
Hour to hour as if it were stitch to stitch

Calm in the circle of her household gods;
Item, to my sister Elizabeth what she lacks—
The courage to gamble on the doubtful odds

And in the end a retreat among Irish lakes
And farmyard smells and the prism of the Irish air;
Item, to Dan my son whenever he wakes

To the consciousness of what his limits are
I leave the ingenuity to transmute
His limits into roads and travel far;

Lastly to Mary living in a remote
Country I leave whatever she would remember
Of hers and mine before she took that boat,

Such memories not being necessarily lumber
And may no chance, unless she wills, delete them
And may her hours be gold and without number.

W. I leave my parents first, seeing that without them
    There's no fame or affection I could win at all
    Whatever fame my poems may collect about them.

    The Royal College of Physicians in Pall Mall
    And a chair in Preventive Medicine, I leave my
        father,
    And the Bewcastle Cross I bequeath to him as well.

    The Church of Saint Aidan at Smallheath to my
        mother
    Where she may pray for this poor world and me,
    And a paying farm to Bernard, my eldest brother.

    Item, to John, my second, my library
    And may my lifetime's luck fall on his head
    That he may walk on Everest before he die.

    Next Edward Upward and Christopher Isherwood
    I here appoint my joint executors
    To judge my work if it be bad or good.

    My manuscripts and letters, all to be theirs
    All copyrights and royalties therefrom
    I leave them as their property in equal shares.

W. L. We leave to Stanley Baldwin, our beloved P.M.,
       The false front of Lincoln Cathedral, and a school
       Of Empire poets. As for his Cabinet, to them

       We leave their National character and strength of
           will.
       To Winston Churchill Ballinrobe's dry harbour
       And Randolph, un bel pezzo, in a codicil.

       To Sir Maurice Hankey for his secretarial labour
       The Vicar of Bray's discretion; and to Lord Lloyd
       We leave a flag-day and a cavalry sabre.

To Vickers the Gran Chaco (for agents must be paid),
The Balkan Conscience and the sleepless night we
  think
The inevitable diseases of their dangerous trade.

The stones of Kaldidalur to Hambro's Bank
And the soapworks in the County of Cheshire we
  gladly grant
To Ramsay MacDonald who's so lucid and frank.

To the Church of England Austen Leigh, The Quantum Theory, Stanford in B flat and the Chief Scout's
  horn
A curate's bicycle, and a portable second hand font.

A Year's subscription to the Gospel Magazine
With which is incorporated the Protestant Deacon,
And a Gentle Shepherd hat but not too clean

We leave the Nonconformists, as a Christmas token,
And all the lives by Franco gently stopped
We leave to Rome, and for the doctrines she has
  spoken

The cock that crew before St. Peter wept.
And to each tribal chief or priestly quack
We leave the treachery of his sect or sept.

Item, to the Bishop of London a hockey-stick
And an Old Marlburian blazer; item to Frank,
The Groupers' Pope, we leave his personal pick

Of a hundred converts from Debrett—we think
Most of them, he will find, have quite a song
Of things to confess from limericks to drink;

Item, we leave to that old diehard Inge
A little Christian joy; item, to Sir
Robert Baden-Powell a piece of string;

Item, to the Primate, pillar of savoir faire,
An exotic entourage; item, to Pat
McCormick a constant audience on the air.

Item, to those who spend their lives in the wet
Lost six counties of the Emerald Isle
We leave our goloshes and a shrimping net;

Item, to Lord Craigavon that old bull
With a horse's face we leave an Orange drum
For after-dinner airs, when he feels full;

Item, to De Valera we leave the dim
Celtic twilight of the higher economics
And a new surname among the seraphim;

Item, to all those Irish whose dynamics
Lead them in circles we leave a cloistered life,
A fellowship say in botany or ceramics.

Item, talking of fellowships, we leave
To that great institution of dreaming spires
With all its lost reputations up its sleeve

A kinder clime for academic careers
Than Thames and Cowley afford, say Medicine Hat
Where petrol fumes will spare the uneasy ears

Of undergraduates growing among the wheat;
And we leave the proctors some powerful opera
     glasses
And half a dozen bulldogs with Lovelock's feet;

Item, to Convocation a bust of Moses,
A lambskin copy of Excerpta de Statutis
And all the howlers of our Latin proses;

Item, to the Oxford O.T.C. our puttees
And to the Oxford Appointments Board some gay
Jobs in Bulawayo or Calaguttis;

Item, to Sir Farquhar Buzzard a raspberry;
Item, to the College of All Souls the game
Of pleonasmus and tautology;

Item, to the Fellows of King's beside the Cam
A bunch of pansies and white violets;
And to all deans and tutors money for jam;

Item, to Wittgenstein who writes such hits
As the Tractatus Logico-Philosophicus
We leave all readers who can spare the wits;

Item, to I. A. Richards who like a mouse
Nibbles linguistics with the cerebral tooth
We leave a quiet evening in a boarding-house

Where he may study the facts of birth and death
In their inexplicable oddity
And put a shilling in the slot for brains and breath.

And Julian Huxley we leave an ant, a bee,
An axolotl and Aldous; item, to Bert-
rand Russell we leave belief in God (D.V.).

Item, we leave a bottle of invalid port
To Lady Astor; item, the Parthenon
On the Calton Hill to Basil de Selincourt.

Item, we leave the phases of the moon
To Mr. Yeats to rock his bardic sleep;
And to Dr. Cyril Norwood a new spittoon;

And Tubby Clayton can have some gingerpop;
And General O'Duffy can take the Harp That Once
Started and somehow was never able to stop.

We leave a mens sana qui mal y pense
To the Public Schools of England, plus Ian Hay
That the sons of gents may have La Plus Bonne
    Chance.

L.   To Marlborough College I leave a lavatory
    With chromium gadgets and the Parthenon frieze;
W. And Holt three broken promises from me.

W. L. Item, to the B.B.C. as a surprise
    The Great Geysir; the Surrealists shall have
    J. A. Smith as an Objet Trouvé in disguise.

To the Royal Academy we leave the 7 and 5
And to the Geological Museum in Jermyn Street
All metaphysicians and logicians still alive.

Item, the Imperial War Museum shall get
Professor Lindemann; and South K. a drove—
In the Science Block the Jeans and Eddington set;

And to the Natural History Wing we give
The reviewers on the *Observer*, the whole damn bunch,
And Beachcomber and the beasts that will not live.

The Dock, in all respect, we leave the Bench
And Shell Mex House we leave to H. G. Wells
To accommodate his spawn of Uebermensch.

Item, to those expert with clubs and balls
And double bores and huntin' and fishin' tackles
Some kippered tigers for their study walls;

To the Fogerty School some tropes of the Reverend
    Tickell's,
And the statue of Peter Pan we leave by halves—
The upper to A. A. Milne, the lower to Beverley
    Nichols.

Last Will and Testament

Item, to Lady Oxford we leave some curves
And a first edition of Dodo; and to that great man
J. L. Garvin the civilisation he deserves.

Item, we leave our old friend Rupert Doone
Something dynamic and his own theatre
And a setting of his Unconscious on the bassoon:

Item, to Daan Hubrecht a Martello tower,
To Hugh M'Diarmid a gallon of Red Biddy,
And the bones of Shakespeare to Sir Archie Flower.

Item, in winter when the ways are muddy
We leave our gumboots tried on Iceland rocks
To the M'Gillicuddy of M'Gillicuddy,

To keep his feet dry climbing in the Reeks:
Item, we leave a portable camping oven
To Norman Douglas, last of the Ancient Greeks;

And to John Fothergill a Corner House in Heaven.
Item, we leave a tube of Pond's Cold Cream
To the débutantes of 1937.

Item, to Maurice Bowra we leave a dome
Of many-coloured glass; item, to Father
Knox a crossword puzzle or a palindrome.

Item, to Compton Mackenzie a sprig of heather,
To James Douglas a knife that will not cut,
And to Roy Campbell a sleeping-suit of leather.

Item, we leave the mentality of the pit
To James Agate and to Ivor Brown,
And to Edith Sitwell we leave her Obiit.

Item, we leave a little simple fun
To all bellettrists and the staff of *Punch*;
And a faith period to Naomi Mitchison.

And to Sir Oswald (please forgive the stench
Which taints our parchment from that purulent
    name)
We leave a rather unpleasant word in French.

Item, we leave to that poor soul A.M.
Ludovici the Venus of Willendorf
(a taste we neither condone nor yet condemn.)

Item, to the King's Proctor and his staff
We leave a skeleton key and *Die Untergang
Des Abendlandes*—a book to make them laugh.

Item, a vestry-meeting to Douglas Byng,
The marriage of universals to Geoffrey Mure,
And Sir James Barrie to Sir Truby King.

And to that Society whose premier law
Is the Preservation of Ancient Monuments
We leave Sir Bindon Blood and Bernard Shaw.

Item, to Dr. Stopes we leave an ounce
Of cocoa-butter and some transcendental love
And may she mix them in the right amounts.

And to the most mischievous woman now alive
We leave a lorry-load of moral mud
And may her Stone Age voodoo never thrive.

And to Evelyn Underhill a diviner's rod;
The Albert Memorial to Osbert Lancaster;
And Messrs. Nervo and Knox to the Eisteddfodd.

And to Ladislas Peri we leave a grand career
As sculptor in concrete, God knows what, or brick;
And Bryan Guinness shall have some Burton beer.

Item, an antidote for camera shock
And a low-brow curiosity in objects to all
Painters and sculptors in metal, wood, or rock.

To modern architects who can design so well
Kitchens and bathrooms, a gentle reminder that
Material pangs are not the only pains of Hell.

To all the technique that composers now have got
We add a feeling for the nature of the human voice
And the love of a tune which sometimes they have
    not.

To our fellow writers, to the whole literary race
The Interest itself in all its circumstances
That each may see his vision face to face.

To our two distinguished colleagues in confidence,
To Stephen Spender and Cecil Day Lewis, we assign
Our minor talents to assist in the defence

Of the European Tradition and to carry on
The Human heritage. [W.] And the Slade School
    I choose
For William Coldstream to leave his mark upon.

W. L. To the Group Theatre that has performed our plays
    We leave the proceeds of the Entertainment Tax
    To pay for sets, and actors on week-days.

W.   To the Post Office Film Unit, a film on Sex
    And to Grierson, its director, something really big
    To sell, I offer with my thanks and my respects.

For my friend Benjamin Britten, composer, I beg
That fortune send him soon a passionate affair.
W. L. To Barbara Hepworth, sculptress, we leave Long
    Meg

And her nine daughters. A pure form, very pure,
We leave Clive Bell, and to Ben Nicolson a post
At Murphy's where he'll soon make good, we're
    sure.

May the critic I. M. Parsons feel at last
A creative impulse, and may the Dictatorship
Of the Holy Spirit suppress the classic past

Of Herbert Read. To Peter Fleming a cap
For exploration. We find him very jolly
But think mock modesty does not improve a chap.

We leave the Martyr's Stake at Abergwilly
To Wyndham Lewis with a box of soldiers (blonde)
Regretting one so bright should be so silly.

We hope one honest conviction may at last be
    found
For Alexander Korda and the Balcon Boys
And the Stavisky Scandal in picture and sound

We leave to Alfred Hitchcock with sincerest praise
Of *Sabotage*. To Berthold Viertel just the script
For which he's waited all his passionate days.

We wish the cottage at Piccadilly Circus kept
For a certain novelist, to write thereon
The spiritual cries at which he's so adept.

To Lord Berners, wit, to keep his memory green
The follies of fifty counties upon one condition
That he write the history of the King and Queen.

L.   And I to all my friends would leave a ration
Of bread and wit against the days which slant
Upon us black with nihilistic passion.

239

Last Will and Testament

Item I leave my old friend Anthony Blunt
A copy of Marx and £1000 a year
And the picture of Love Locked Out by Holman
    Hunt.

Item to Archie Burton I leave my car
Which took the count at a crossroads in King's
    Heath
And bringing me twice in jeopardy at the bar

All but left me a convict or a wraith;
Item I leave a large viridian pot
Of preserved ginger to my dear Ann Faith

Shepard who shall also have my Bokhara mat
And Graham Shepard shall have my two cider mugs,
My thirty rose-trees and, if he likes, my hat.

Item I leave my copies of *Our Dogs*
To Mrs. Norton who lives at Selly Hill:
And to Victor Rothschild the spermatozoa of frogs.

Item my golf clubs to Ernest Ludwig Stahl
Which after a little treatment with emery paper
Should serve him well around the veldt and kraal;

And Vera Stahl his sister I leave an upper
Seat at Twickenham for the Irish match
To be followed by a very récherché supper.

And Mrs. Dodds I leave a champion bitch
And a champion dog and a litter of champion pups
All to be born and weaned without a hitch:

And Professor Dodds I leave the wind which whips
The Dublin Mountains and the Knockmealdowns
And may he forgive my academic slips.

Last Will and Testament

Item to Betsy my borzoi a dish of bones
And 7/6 for her licence for next year
And may her name be scratched on the Abbey stones:

Item to Littleton Powys more and more
I leave my admiration and all the choice
Flowers and birds that grace our English shore.

Item to Wilfred Blunt a pretty piece
Of the best rococo and a crimson shirt
Appliquéd all over with fleurs-de-lys:

Item to J. R. Hilton a Work of Art
And a dream of the infinitesimal calculus
Bolstered on apples in an apple-cart.

Item to Mr. and Mrs. McCance a mouse
That will keep their cats in one perpetual smile:
Item to Moore Crosthwaite a concrete house

Built by Gropius: item to George Morell
Perpetual luck at the dogs: item to Tom
Robinson a blue check homer that flies like hell

And makes his fortune: item a quiet room
To Denis Binyon to practise his Hellenistic
Greek in readiness for the Day of Doom:

W. L. Item to dear John Waterhouse a gymnastic
Exercise before breakfast every day
(A better cure for the figure than wearing elastic)

And a grand piano under a flowering tree
To sate his versatile and virile taste
From the Hammerklavier to the Isle of Capri.

Item to Gordon Herrickx a titan's wrist
Strong to the evening from commercial stone
And may his glyptic fantasy persist:

241

Item, to Robert Medley some cellophane
And a pack of jokers; item, a box of talc
To Geoffrey Tandy in case he shaves again.

Item to Humphrey Thackrah a flowered silk
Dressing-gown and a bottle of Numero Cinq:
Item to Isiah Berlin a saucer of milk:

L.   Item to Lella Sargent Florence a drink
After hours and a salad of chicory:
Item to my cousin Oonagh a coat of mink:

Item to the Brothers Melville the artist's eye
And may their beliefs not hamper them for ever:
Item to Guy Morgan and also Guy

Burgess and Ben Bonas and Hector MacIver
And Robert Dunnett and Norman Cameron
I leave a keg of whiskey, the sweet deceiver:

Item I leave to my old friend Adrian
Green Armitage who now is a stockbroker,
A jolly life as an English gentleman:

Item to Helen Cooke I leave an acre
Of Cornish moor to run her spaniels in
On perfect terms with the local butcher and baker:

Item I leave a sun which will always shine
To Elspeth Duxbury and a ginger cat
Which will always be washed and groomed by half-
    past nine:

Item to Ivan Rowe a gallon pot
Of Stephens' blue-black ink: item to Walter
Allen I leave the tale of a tiny tot

On the Midland Regional and from the welter
Of hand-to-mouth journalism and graft
I hope his brains afford him sufficient shelter:

Item to Edith Marcuse I leave a deft
Hand at designing and an adequate job,
And to Coral Brown camellias on her right and left.

Item to Mrs. Hancock a koala cub:
Item to Cicely Russell and R. D. Smith
The joint ownership of a Shropshire pub:

Item to Bernard and Nora Spencer a path
To a life of colour, ample and debonair:
Item to old John Bowle a Turkish bath:

Item to Diana Sanger an open fire
A wire fox terrier and a magnolia tree;
And to Ruthven Todd the works of Burns entire.

Item to Curigwen Lewis the Broadway sky
Blazing her name in lights; item to Jack
Chase my best regards and a case of rye:

Item to C. B. Canning a private joke:
Item a clerihew to Christopher Holme
And may he not be always completely broke:

Item to David Gretton a lovely time
Arranging broadcasts from the Parish Hall:
Item to May Lawrence a gin and lime:

Item to Francis Curtis, once Capel,
I leave my wonder at his Oxford Past
Which to my knowledge was without parallel:

W. L. Item to John Betjeman (the most
    Remarkable man of his time in any position)
    We leave a Leander tie and Pugin's ghost

And a box of crackers and St. Pancras Station
And the *Church of Ireland Gazette* and our
    confidence
That he will be master of every situation.

A Chinese goose to Harold Acton we advance.
W.   Item my passport to Heinz Nedermeyer
And to John Andrews, to rub with after a dance,

As many L.M.S. towels as he may require.
W. L. Item to E. M. Forster a bright new notion
For a novel with a death roll, O dear, even higher.

And to St. John Ervine, ornament of the nation,
His Ulster accent and les neiges d'antan
And a little, if possible, accurate information:

And some new games with time to J. W. Dunne,
To Andy Corry a six-foot belemnite,
And to Noel Coward a place in the setting sun;

To Dylan Thomas a leek on a gold plate;
Item we leave to that great mind Charles Madge
Some curious happenings to correlate;

Item to the *New Statesman* a constant grudge
And a constant smile saying 'We told you so',
And to John Sparrow a quarter of a pound of
    fudge.

Item, the falling birthrate we leave to Roy
Harrod and Maynard Keynes for pulling together;
To Brian Howard a watch and the painted buoy

That dances at the harbour mouth (which is rather
The poésie de départs but sooner or later
We all like being trippers); item to Father

244

  D'Arcy, that dialectical disputer,
  We leave St. Thomas Aquinas and his paeans—
W. To Neville Coghill, fellow of Exeter, my tutor,

  I leave Das Lebendigste with which to form
   alliance
  And to Professor Dawkins who knows the Modern
   Greeks
  I leave the string figure called the Fighting Lions.

W. L. To the barrister, Richard Best, to wear on walks
  A speckled boater; to Geoffrey Grigson of *New Verse*
  A strop for his sharp tongue before he talks.

  A terrible double entendre in metre or in prose
  To William Empson; and we leave his own
  Post mortem to any doctor who thinks he knows

W. The Inmost Truth. And the New Peace he has won
  To Gerald Heard—and to the teacher Maurice Feild
  A brilliant pupil as reward for all he's done.

  To Geoffrey Hoyland, whose virtues are manifold
  An equal love for every kind of nature,
W. L. And to John Davenport a permanent job to hold.

W. For Peggy Garland someone real in every feature,
  To Tom her husband, someone to help; and a call
  To go a dangerous mission for a fellow creature

  To Nancy Coldstream. I hope John Layard will
  Find quick ones always to put him on his feet
  To Olive Mangeot a good lodger and, till

  The revolution cure her corns, a set
  Of comfortable shoes: to Sylvain, her younger son,
  My suits to wear when it is really wet.

My Morris-Cowley to carry chickens in
To Peter Roger, with a very fine large goat.
And a Healer's Prize for Robert Moody to win.

W. L. We leave with our best compliments the Isle of Wight
To Robert Graves and Laura Riding, because
An Italian island is no good place to write.

We leave to the Inland Revenue Commissioners
The Channel Islands: for these charming men
Will find there many an undeserving purse.

W. I leave the wheel at Laxey, Isle of Man,
To Sean Day-Lewis, and the actual island leave
To Mrs Yates of Brooklands, to rest there when she
can.

W. L. The County of Surrey as it stands we give
To Sapper; and all the roadhouses in Herts
To Hilaire Belloc that he may drink and live.

To Quinton Hogg the wardenship of the Cinque
Ports,
And the holy double well of Saint Clether to all
Who suffer guilty feelings and irrational thoughts.

To Sebastian Sprott we offer Mortimer's Hole
W. To snub-nosed Gabriel Carritt the Beetle and Wedge
And T.F.C. may keep the letter that he stole.

W. L. To Mayfair, Crowland Abbey's river-lacking bridge
As symbol of its life. To Crossman, Councillor,
We leave High Office, and a wind-swept northern
ridge.

We leave to Cowper Powys Glastonbury Tor
The White Horses to the Horse Guards, and the
vale of Evenlode
To all those shell-shocked in the last Great War.

        For Pacifists to keep the brutal world outside
        We've Offa's Dyke, and the caves at Castleton for
            parents
        Who dream of air-raids and want a place to hide.

        Item, we leave to Professor Sargant Florence
        Dartington Hall and all that is therein.
        And Dartmoor Prison to Sir Herbert Pethick
            Lawrence.

W.   To Rex Warner, birdman, I leave Wicken Fen
        And Hillborough Dovecote. To Sydney Newman
            give
        The Coronation Organ to play now and then.

W. L. The twin towers of the Crystal Palace we would
            leave
        To Leonard and Virginia Woolf, and Boston Stump
        To Ernest Jones, round which they each may weave

        Their special phantasies. To every tramp
        We leave a harvest barn, a private drive
        And a fenced deer park where he may make his
            camp.

        Snowdonia to Michael Roberts with our love,
        To Constant Lambert the Three Choirs Festival,
        And the Vale of Eden with the Pennine scarp above

        To the children of the London East End. Sweet
            Boars Hill
        To Poets Laureate, past, present, and to come.
        As for the parts of our bodies in this will

        We allot them here as follows: to the Home
        For Lost Dogs and Cats our livers and lights,
        And our behinds to the Birmingham Hippodrome.

And our four eyes which cannot see for nuts
We leave to all big-game hunters and to all
Apprentices to murder at the butts;

Our feet to hikers when their own feet fail;
To all escapists our islands of Langahans;
And to Imperial Chemicals a pail

Of what in us would otherwise join the drains;
The Watch Committee can have our noses and
The British Association can have our brains;

Item our ears, apt for the slightest sound,
We leave those Statesmen who happen to be de-
        barred
From hearing how the wheels of State run round;

To Major Yogi-Brown our navels we award
And our pudenda we leave or rather fling
Our biographers and The Thames Conservancy
        Board;

Lastly our hearts, whether they be right or wrong,
We leave neither to scientists nor doctors
But to those to whom they properly belong.

Our grit we beg to leave all sanitary inspectors,
Our faith, our hope, our charity we leave The
        League
To help it to do something in the future to protect us.

Our cheerfulness to each square-headed peg
That lives in a round hole, and our charm at its best
To those who cannot dig and are ashamed to beg.

Our powers of parrot memory we offer to assist
Examinees. Our humour, all we think is funny,
To Dr. Leavis and almost every psycho-analyst.

To the Bishop of Bradford our discretion, if any;
And our carnivorous appetites we give away
To Professor Gilbert Murray. Item, our many

Faults to all parents that their families may see
No one expects them really to be good as gold.
After due thought, we leave our lust in Chancery,

Our obstinacy to the untamed and wild.
W.   I leave to my ex-pupils whether bright or dull
Especially to every homesick problem child

All the good times I've had since I left school.
And hope that Erika, my wife, may have her wish
To see the just end of Hitler and his unjust rule.

W. L. To all the dictators who look so bold and fresh
      The midnight hours, the soft wind from the sweep-
         ing wing
      Of madness, and the intolerable tightening of the
         mesh

Of history. We leave their marvellous native tongue
To Englishmen, and for our intelligent island pray
That to her virtuous beauties by all poets sung

She add at last an honest foreign policy.
For her oppressed, injured, insulted, and weak
The logic and the passion proper for victory.

We leave our age the quite considerable spark
Of private love and goodness which never leaves
An age, however awful, in the utter dark.

We leave the unconceived and unborn lives
A closer approximation to real happiness
Than has been reached by us, our neighbours or
      their wives.

To those who by office or from inclination use
Authority, a knowledge of their own misdeed
And all the hate that coercion must produce.

For the lost who from self-hatred cannot hide,
Such temporary refuge or engines of escape
From pain as Chance and Mercy can provide

And to the good who know how wide the gulf, how
    deep
Between Ideal and Real, who being good have felt
The final temptation to withdraw, sit down and
    weep,

We pray the power to take upon themselves the guilt
Of human action, though still as ready to confess
The imperfection of what can and must be built,
The wish and power to act, forgive, and bless.

Epilogue

For W. H. Auden

Now the winter nights begin
Lonely comfort walls me in;
So before the memory slip
I review our Iceland trip—

Not for me romantic nor
Idyll on a mythic shore
But a fancy turn, you know,
Sandwiched in a graver show.

Down in Europe Seville fell,
Nations germinating hell,
The Olympic games were run—
Spots upon the Aryan sun.

And the don in me set forth
How the landscape of the north
Had educed the saga style
Plodding forward mile by mile.

And the don in you replied
That the North begins inside,
Our ascetic guts require
Breathers from the Latin fire.

So although no ghost was scotched
We were happy while we watched

Epilogue

Ravens from their walls of shale
Cruise around the rotting whale,

Watched the sulphur basins boil,
Loops of steam uncoil and coil,
While the valley fades away
To a sketch of Judgment Day.

So we rode and joked and smoked
With no miracles evoked,
With no levitations won
In the thin unreal sun;

In that island never found
Visions blossom from the ground,
No conversions like St. Paul,
No great happenings at all.

Holidays should be like this,
Free from over-emphasis,
Time for soul to stretch and spit
Before the world comes back on it,

Before the chimneys row on row
Sneer in smoke, 'We told you so'
And the fog-bound sirens call
Ruin to the long sea-wall.

Rows of books around me stand,
Fence me round on either hand;
Through that forest of dead words
I would hunt the living birds—

Great black birds that fly alone
Slowly through a land of stone,
And the gulls who weave a free
Quilt of rhythm on the sea.

Here in Hampstead I sit late
Nights which no one shares and wait
For the 'phone to ring or for
Unknown angels at the door;

Better were the northern skies
Than this desert in disguise—
Rugs and cushions and the long
Mirror which repeats the song.

For the litany of doubt
From these walls comes breathing out
Till the room becomes a pit
Humming with the fear of it

With the fear of loneliness
And uncommunicableness;
All the wires are cut, my friends
Live beyond the severed ends.

So I write these lines for you
Who have felt the death-wish too,
But your lust for life prevails—
Drinking coffee, telling tales.

Our prerogatives as men
Will be cancelled who knows when;
Still I drink your health before
The gun-butt raps upon the door.

L. M.

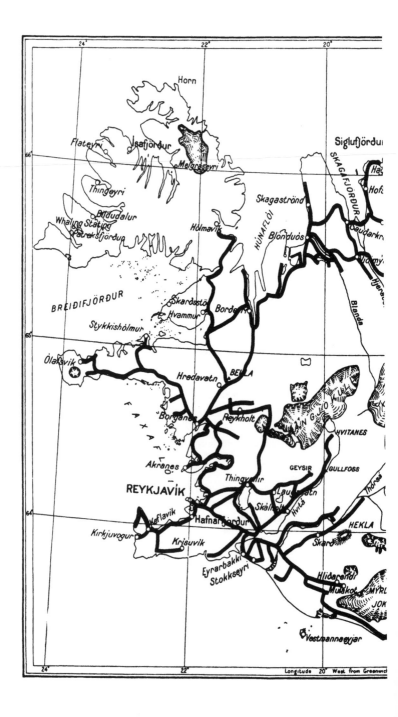

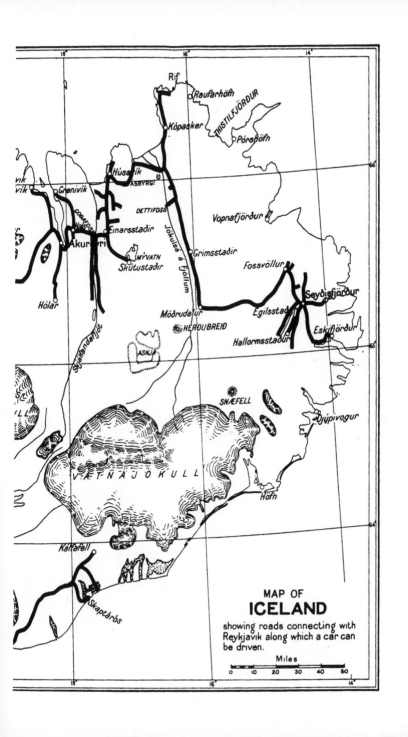

MAP OF
ICELAND

showing roads connecting with
Reykjavík along which a car can
be driven.

Miles

0   10   20   30   40   50

7154138R00142

Printed in Great Britain
by Amazon.co.uk, Ltd.,
Marston Gate.